CAREER PLANNING

JOBS & CAREERS

CAREER PLANNING FOR WOMEN

How to make a positive impact
on your working life

Laurel Alexander

How To Books

By the same author in this series

Surviving Redundancy
Finding a Job with a Future

Cartoons by Mike Flanagan

British Library Cataloguing in Publication Data
A catalogue record for this book is available from the British Library.

First published in 1996 by How To Books Ltd, Plymbridge House,
Estover Road, Plymouth PL6 7PZ, United Kingdom.
Tel: Plymouth (01752) 202301. Fax: (01752) 202331.

Note: The material contained in this book is set out in good faith for
general guidance and no liability can be accepted for loss or expense
incurred as a result of relying in particular circumstances on statements
made in the book. The laws and regulations are complex and liable to
change, and readers should check the current position with the relevant
authorities before making personal arrangements.

Produced for How To Books by Deer Park Productions
Typeset by Concept Communications, (Design & Print) Ltd, Crayford, Kent.
Printed and bound by Cromwell Press, Broughton Gifford, Melksham, Wiltshire.

Contents

List of Illustrations

Preface

This book is for women in or out of work. If you are returning to work after a career break or bringing up a family, if you have been made redundant or are seeking a career change – this book will help you re-focus your aims and objectives.

But the book is also written with men in mind. One of the primary objectives is to present a wider picture of the changing face of work as seen from the woman's point of view, working alongside men. So this book is also for the men who can foresee the evolution of women in the workplace and who want to encourage the changes that lie ahead for us all.

By looking to the future and observing the reshaping of work trends, we can begin to challenge the problems of women at work. This book covers issues such as empowerment, confidence building, developing the right skills, career planning, training in jobs for the future, using female qualities in business development, moving into management, dealing with sexual harassment and time management.

Men and women have different approaches to work because we think, communicate, make decisions, take risks and manage in unique ways. However, these differences can complement each other when we understand and accept that each gender has its own specialities.

This book will help women to understand themselves and men to understand women.

Laurel Alexander

IS THIS YOU?

Returning to work   Facing redundancy

Unemployed

Seeking a change of direction   Moving into management

Seeking confidence

Looking for a new way to work   Looking for a career plan

Breaking away from stereotype jobs

Wanting to contribute to the workplace   Becoming empowered

Looking to raise your self-esteem

Developing assertiveness   Developing leadership skills

Developing presentation skills

Leaving school   Going for an interview

Becoming self-employed

Thinking about training   Seeking new responsibilities

Challenging prejudice at work

Leaving college   Dealing with sexual harassment

Coping with change

Dealing with anxiety   Overcoming physical tension

Thinking positively

Managing your time effectively   Developing a work strategy

Facing promotion

Seeking to balance   Looking for a successful
home and career   working life

1
Looking to the Future for Working Women

Did you know:

- women make up 52 per cent of the world's population

- women do 60 per cent of the world's work

- women receive less than 10 per cent of salaries?

RESHAPING WORK TRENDS

According to the Institute of Careers Guidance and Centre for Research in Employment and Technology in Europe, future trends in the labour market include:

- an increase in the female workforce as a majority of new jobs go to women

- a concern for the natural environment, individualism, business ethics, local community life and a greater sense of trust and co-operation with alliances and networking (these are traditionally female orientated values)

- more women acquiring professional qualifications

- more employers recognising women as a vital resource

- women increasingly entering skills-intensive, white collar jobs.

PLANNING YOUR CAREER

According to the same institute, we need to be aware of several areas of development if we wish to remain in employment:

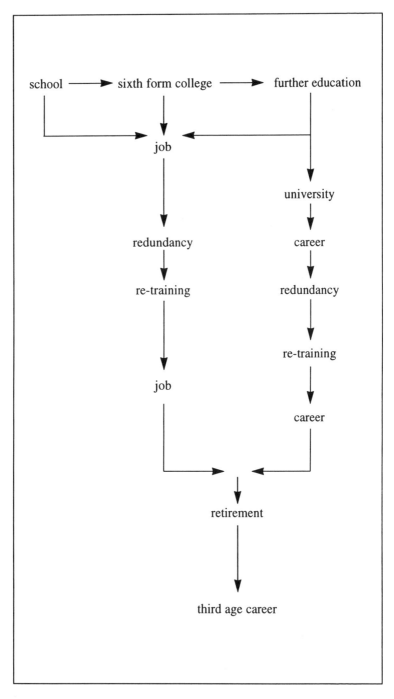

Fig. 1. The working pattern.

- planning for multiple careers

- evolving a life-time career plan

- developing job-specific skills

- building up personal development skills

- enlarging professional development skills

- involving yourself in a continuous learning programme.

Planning for multiple careers
The average **career** now lasts for five years before we have to consider a sideways move or re-training. Gone are the days of a job for life. With social and economic changes, we can expect to experience the pattern shown in Figure 1.

We need to be aware of **multi-skilling** ourselves so that we have a 'toolbox' of skills, knowledge and experience to transfer to other occupations.

Evolve a life-time career plan
In order to maintain a feeling of control, we need to have a flexible **career plan** (see Figure 2). A career plan should be open to constant change.

DEVELOPING SKILLS

Job-specific skills development

- *Procedural*: The awareness, knowledge and application of routine and non-routine tasks.

- *Technological*: The ability to design, develop or operate information systems.

Personal development skills

- *Interpersonal*: Being able to communicate with professionals, customers, clients and colleagues effectively using written, oral and non-verbal skills.

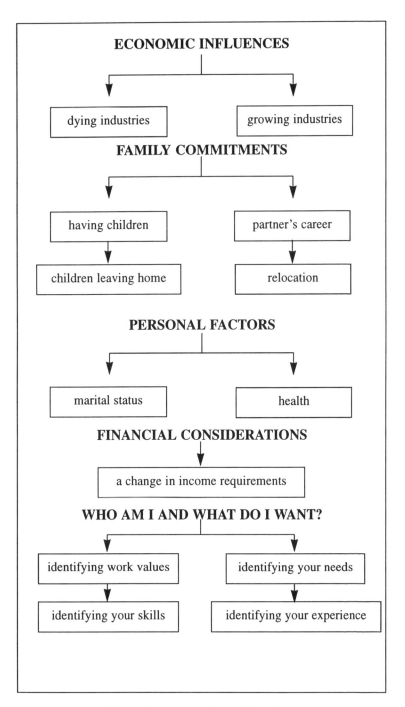

Fig. 2. Your career plan considerations.

Professional development skills

- *Knowledge-based*: Knowledge that is job related. Also the process of logical thought and interpretation which relates events into meaningful patterns.

- *Entrepreneurial*: The efficient use of resources, the ability to pursue goals and a pro-active stance.

- *Flexibility*: The willingness to take risks, change direction and take advantage of opportunities.

- *Diversification*: To develop continuously an awareness of all-round vision, to be knowledgeable about the changing face of industry and commerce and to build many levels of skills and knowledge.

Involve yourself in a continuous learning programme

Education
A broad-based early education is a vital foundation for later training. Young people can now be prepared for GNVQs (General National Vocational Qualifications), which offer a base for employment.

On-the-job training
More and more companies are offering their staff training opportunities and it is to your benefit to take advantage of these courses and workshops. The training may be delivered by management or trainers employed by the company or by outside trainers called in for specialised delivery. The training may be job-specific, professional or personal.

Off-the-job training
You could take the initiative and develop a training programme for yourself. You will have to bear the cost if you are working. If you choose to do your training this way, it is very much under your control. If you are looking for a course, you could contact your local TAPS (Training and Access Point).
   Note: If you are claiming benefit, you may be eligible for free training to a qualification standard. Ask at your local Jobcentre.

Develop transferable skills between occupations rather than industries
As you build your portfolio of skills, knowledge and experience, it

would be helpful to bear in mind the importance of **transferable skills**. That is developing a skill which could be used in a number of occupations, *eg* word processing skills could be used in secretarial work, desk top publishing, writing or running your own business.

Choose employers who facilitate continuous learning
Employers who facilitate continuous learning in their staff are the employers of the future. They see their staff as their prime resource and are prepared to work with you. If you are motivated and interested, the company is going to get more productivity and a higher level of efficiency from you.

Getting out of the 'school' way of thinking
You may have experienced school as being restricting, authoritarian and boring. Vocational training today is very different. Sitting in the classroom, learning by theory, is becoming obsolete. Training for work is about gaining skills as part of work experience. Theory is interpreted into knowledge, skills and application. You are no longer a child, you are an adult – expected to query and interpret according to your own experience.

NEW WAYS TO WORK
According to the Institute of Careers Guidance and Centre for Research in Employment and Technology in Europe:

- the number of part-time jobs held by women will increase markedly

- self-employment amongst women will increase modestly.

Other ways in which you might consider arranging your working life include:

- *flexitime*: a regular core of hours taken between a flexible time span

- *temping*: an excellent way of gaining a wide span of experience in a variety of environments without the commitment; also a way of earning while you consider a change of career

- *jobshare*: a full-time job shared between two people

- *contract work*: short- or long-term contracts for a specified time period

- *interim management*: contract work for executives and professionals to work on a specified project

- *teleworking*: working for a company at home using computers, modem, telephone and fax

- *term-time working*: working during term-time only.

BECOMING SELF-EMPLOYED

According to a survey by *Home Run* magazine (1995):

- a high percentage of women run businesses linked to writing, journalism, sales and marketing, business services or training

- a high percentage of self-employed women are in the 30-49 age group

- the main advantages of working from home include flexibility, no travel or commuting, independence and low costs

- the main disadvantages include lack of contact with others, domestic interruptions, being always on call and lack of interaction.

Do you want to:

- achieve your full potential

- take whatever risks you like

- work the hours you want

- improve your confidence

- avoid being unemployed

- work at something you enjoy

- make unlimited money

- learn about business?

Figure 3 will give you an idea of what you might need.

Business tasks	Skills and knowledge involved
MARKET RESEARCH	Identify client group. Identify their reasons for buying. Clarify how your customers/clients will buy. Make sure your market is a growth area. Research your competitors.
BUSINESS PLANNING	Will your business take diversification? Can you expand your business idea in time? Is your business flexible? Can you control your cash flow?
FINANCIAL CONTROL	Keeping accounting books. Debt chasing and credit control. Drawing up budgets. Raising capital. Establishing prices.
MARKETING/SALES	Advertising. Public relations. Selling.
STOCK CONTROL	Product distribution.
MANAGEMENT	Recruiting staff. Project management. Team building.
LEGALITIES	Establishing your business identity. Registration of patents, copyright or trade mark. Renting or leasing business premises. Obtaining licences. Obtaining insurance. Registering for VAT. Informing the Inland Revenue. Informing the DSS.

Fig. 3. The self-employment checklist.

Checklist

1. If you want to re-evaluate your career, see a careers counsellor (*Yellow Pages*).

2. To increase your job-specific skills or professional development skills, take an NVQ or if working, ask for on-the-job training.

3. To increase your interpersonal skills, look in your local adult education prospectus.

4. To develop a continuous learning programme, keep yourself informed of training where you work and if applicable, join an institute relevant to your profession.

5. If you want to become self-employed, contact your local Training and Enterprise Council for help.

CASE STUDIES

Maria doesn't know what she wants

Maria is 23, single and ambitious for something better and more exciting. She left school in 1988 and built up her secretarial and administration skills with ease. Since then, she has found it very difficult getting and keeping a job and has taken several temporary positions as a secretary. She doesn't really want to carry on as a secretary, but doesn't know what she wants to do, apart from having a good time and not getting tied down. Her mother has worked as a secretary in the same firm for 20 years and her father is a self-employed builder. Maria has an older sister who works abroad as a translator.

Carol changes her career

Carol is in her mid 30s, married with one child. She began her working life in catering, married and worked her way up to management level. Redundancy struck and Carol found she was ready for a complete change. She chose the Civil Service.

Diane is at a crossroads

Diane is 48 and divorced with two children. She left school in the early 1960s to work in a printer's bindery. She had two career breaks when she had her children. When she was 40, the marriage broke up.

DISCUSSION POINTS

1. What could the benefits of being a 'portfolio' person (*ie* having two or three careers running simultaneously) be for you?

2. Why are interpersonal skills becoming more important in the workplace? What has been your experience of customer care, as a customer?

3. Why are women becoming an increasing force in the workplace?

2
Identifying the Female Role Model

CHALLENGING THE PROBLEMS OF WOMEN AT WORK

Women, more than ever before, are re-formulating and re-focusing their place in society. Traditional stereotypes are being challenged as we step into a second industrial revolution. Today, women have new opportunities to define themselves through paid work as more women return to the workplace and take the option of a career.

In the light of a new, emerging workforce, certain issues need addressing:

● for the career-minded woman, there are few female role models within the working environment

● women find their personal power hard to handle because it has not been used openly

● assertive women at work can acquire the unwelcome labels of being bossy and hard-nosed

● some men are not necessarily used to being led by women

● women are uncomfortable about getting on the promotion ladder

● sexual harassment is still a major issue

● most working women still see themselves as having to do and be everything to everybody

● many positions of power in business are held by men who are prejudiced against women

● some women try to prove themselves either by putting men down, thereby creating more prejudice, or by trying to be like men, thereby creating resentment.

In order to re-define women's roles at work for the future, we need to explore the foundation upon which our beliefs and behaviours are built.

UNDERSTANDING OUR SELF-IMAGE

In general, we all are subject to influence by other people. As women, we accept additional judgements, placed upon us by external sources. In effect, we are often our own worst enemy. Consequently, the rise of feminism has fostered a belief that equality means putting men down, so that women can get on top. This in turn has confused everybody. Men, because they are facing a gender revolution as their roles change. Women, because they believe they have to think and act like men in order to be accepted as equal. Most women seem reluctant to accept responsibility for themselves, preferring instead to be a victim and blaming men or other women. Maybe the issue shouldn't be about equality, but about accepting and respecting the qualities of each gender without prejudice.

The image women have of themselves is confused, multi-faceted and compounded by social development, politics and the media. Women tend to respond to these external pressures which are built onto childhood conditioning and early female role models.

Using labels

Image is built on the labels we use for ourselves and each other. People label each other in order to maintain some sense of order and control. We label by:

- gender
- age
- appearance
- the area in which we live
- job
- accent
- the condition and appearance of our house
- where we take our holidays
- car
- how our children behave
- where we had our schooling
- whether we rent or have a mortgage

- star sign
- religious beliefs
- nationality
- skin colour.

We label each other for safety. We know where we are – what to expect. When we label, we make judgements, often inaccurately and with prejudice. When we accept someone else's label, we are accepting their opinion of us.

Labels

What image do each of these labels conjure up for you? How do they make you feel?

- woman
- bossy
- hysteric
- catty
- iron lady
- moody
- feminine
- indecisive.

Hiding behind the masks

A crucial part of women re-defining their needs and wants is to understand the roles they play in life – the masks they hide behind. We play so many parts in our life, that the real me, the true self is hidden, afraid to come out from behind mummy's skirts. It is important to identify the masks we wear so that we can begin to:

- understand the various parts of our nature

- admit the masks we use to conveniently hide behind

- celebrate the masks we truly enjoy

- discard the marks we resent.

Exercise

1. Take a large piece of paper and put the word ME in the centre.

accountant	crisis-maker	hoarder	negotiator
actress	critic	home-builder	neurotic
administrator	crusader	humanitarian	new age woman
admirer	cynic	hysteric	nice-as-pie
adventurer	deadbeat	idealist	nun
adviser	denier	immovable rock	optimist
aggressor	destroyer	inquirer	overdoer
analyst	dissector	insane	parasite
angel	dissenter	intellectual	peacemaker
appreciator	doer	investigator	perfectionist
artist	dogmatist	iron maiden	performer
athlete	doubter	jealous bitch	pessimist
aunt	drifter	judge	petty tyrant
bad girl	drunk	killer	philosopher
bargain-hunter	egotist	know-it-all	pleaser
big momma	elusive	leader	poet
big sister	entertainer	listener	powerhouse
big spender	entrepreneur	live wire	pretender
bookworm	escapist	logician	procrastinator
boss	evaluator	loner	protector
braggart	excitement addict	loser	provider
brooder	extremist	lost soul	psychic
bulldozer	fairy-godmother	lover	psychologist
bum	fighter	mad hatter	puritan
businesswoman	fixer	Madonna	queen bee
busy bee	flatterer	manager	realist
catalyst	flirt	martyr	rebel
chameleon	free soul	materialist	reformer
charmer	friend	menial	reliable plodder
chauffeur	genius	messenger	rescuer
child	gentle dove	ministering angel	risk-taker
Cinderella	glutton	miser	romantic
clingy	gossiper	misfit	saleswoman
co-operator	gourmet	miss bubbly	Santa Claus
comforter	groupie	miss empathy	schemer
comic	grudge bearer	miss humility	scientist
competitor	guru	missionary	secretary
computer	harassed executive	mistress	seducer
conformist	harassed	money-maker	seer
confronter	housewife	moralist	self-indulger
controller	healer	mother	sensualist
cook	health fanatic	mother earth	sex kitten
counsellor	heretic	musician	sex maniac
country girl	heroine	mystifier	show-off
creator	hippie	needy	shy violet

Fig. 4. Masks that I wear.

sister	status seeker	victim	wife
slob	stoic	VIP	willing horse
social butterfly	student	vulnerable	winner
softie	taker	walking	witch
spirit	teddy bear	encyclopaedia	withholder
spoiled brat	tester	wallower	workaholic
sponge	tragedy queen	wanderer	worrier
sportswoman	ugly duckling	weirdo	
star	uncommitted	whore	

Using all the sheet, write down all the masks you identify with, using Figure 4 as a prompt.

2. On a separate sheet, mark three columns. In column one, write the masks you use to conveniently hide behind. In column two, write the masks you enjoy and in column three, write the marks you resent.

Looking at beliefs

Labels arise from our belief system. Our beliefs are largely stored in our subconscious and become a reality through our life experiences. Our own belief system is formed as a result of other people's beliefs combined with the circumstances of our past. In order to survive, we had to adopt to the beliefs of our family and society's expectations. These beliefs include the rules and negative messages that we were taught and thus incorporated into our view of ourselves and others. Our beliefs may include:

● A woman shouldn't run a business.

● Women should have babies.

● Women are hysterical.

● Women shouldn't be ambitious.

● It's not feminine to get angry.

● A woman's place is in the home.

● It isn't right for a woman to want a career.

● Women should earn less than their partners.

25

Use the spaces below to set out your beliefs.

My beliefs
What do I believe about myself?

Myself as a woman?

My potential?

My limitations?

Where do these beliefs come from? Have others told me this about myself? Have I developed this belief on my own?

How I see myself
Without too much thought, complete the following:

I am a woman who –

LEARNING THE ROLES

The role of **conditioning** in our lives is crucial to the shaping of our identity. As children, we are dependent upon adults to feed, nurture and guide us. We are in their power and they pass onto us their beliefs, values and attitudes. As we grow, we absorb their teachings into our psyche and the subtle blending of external influences and our own internal character makes a heady rulebook for adult life.

Conditioning through external influences

Parents

During our formative years, our parents (or other primary people) provide our initial role models. Mum gives us an idea of what being female is about while dad provides the male approval (or otherwise). There is always the struggle to rebel against our parents or to emulate them. However, we don't necessarily work through issues directly with our parents. Often we deal with them via other indirect sources such as lovers, friends or work colleagues. If, for example, we grew up with a particularly controlling or critical parent, we may rebel against authority figures at work or be constantly seeking approval from them.

As children, we want to be noticed and approved of by our parents and other role models. If we received constant disapproval and criticism when young, as adults we are likely to constantly seek validation from others. Not knowing how to approve of ourselves, by learning through example, can prevent us from discovering our own needs and wants. We look for reactions in others and assume what we must do is to please them. This may result in fearing failure and feeling unworthy, thus holding ourselves back from fulfilment through work (or other life areas).

Uncovering past messages

What do I remember about my mother's attitude towards work?

Did she work?

What did she do? Did she value her work?

What do I remember about my father's attitude towards work? What was his attitude towards women/my mother working?

What messages was I given about work suitable for women when I was about to leave school?

Copying role models

We learn, by example, that men and women think, feel and behave differently. Vive la difference! However, we are also taught that certain differences are limiting. Traditional associations may include:

Male	Female
aggressive	yielding
thrusting	understanding
logical	tender
organised	sympathetic
leader	compassionate
ambitious	affectionate
risk-taker	gentle
self-sufficient	gullible
strong	shy
decisive	vulnerable
independent	wise
forceful	intuitive
dominant	nurturing
competitive	spontaneous
reasoning	receptive
assertive	creative
judgemental	introverted
rigid	spatial
disciplined	soft
protective	emotional

Using male role models

As girls, our role models were primarily gleaned from mother and other female relations, friends, authority figures, film, television, the music world and famous women in the news. Males get their role models from father and other male relations through to men in business, politics, sport etc. There are not many female role models in business to give women a positive sense of how to behave and how much can be achieved.

Because of this lack of female role models, it is tempting for women to use men as a standard to how to think, feel and behave in business. In other words, to become female men. Constructively, we have two choices in selecting role models:

1. Use peer women.

2. Use male role models (be selective from male mentors, integrating positive behaviours in with your own style).

    We use role models through observation and mimicry of:

●   values and beliefs
●   emotional responses
●   communication style
●   behaviour
●   dress.

    If there are no suitable role models to select, this may be to your benefit as there are no criteria against which others can make judgements.

Exercise

1. What key words would you associate with both genders?

2. Which qualities do you find restrictive in your own behaviour?

3. Which qualities do you find irritating in other women?

4. Which qualities do you find irritating in men?

    The qualities that irritate us about others are often qualities we have repressed in ourselves.

Balancing the male and female

Women do not have to browbeat men into submission, stride around in hob-nail boots or shout the odds in order to be seen, heard and respected by others. Women have their unique female qualities which can be useful in the workplace.

Within every woman's psychological make-up dwells what is called the **animus**. The animus represents the male qualities within a female. Every man has the counterpart of an **anima** – the female qualities within a male. The female part (of men and women) intuitively creates the holding bay upon which the male part (of women and men) acts and produces form. (See Figure 5.)

As women, the larger part of our psychological make-up is instinctive

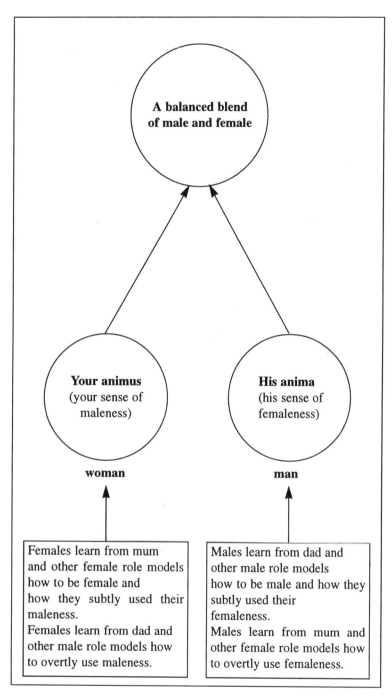

Fig. 5. The male/female balancing act.

and receptive and it is our animus, our male side, which needs to be encouraged out in a positive way and blended with our femaleness. The tendency is to have insight (female) and to act upon it **aggressively** (male) as we observe the male role models around us to do. The healthy way is to have insight and to act upon it **assertively**, referring back to the female for further insight and guidance to produce the right balance.

ESTABLISHING A WORK IDENTITY

The world of work is in a major state of change due to global marketing, major shifts in commerce and industry plus new ways of working such as teleworking, jobshare and flexitime.

We are not our work. We shouldn't hide behind our work, afraid to come out. Just as we shouldn't hide behind motherhood, devastated when the children leave home. Work is only one facet of our self-expression. We can develop self-expression through a continuous learning programme in order to develop skills relevant to the labour market trends. Skills development is one part of a healthy work identity involving:

● knowing our work motivations

● continuous learning

● working for employers that provide continuous learning opportunities

● developing job-specific skills

● developing abstract skills such as assertiveness

● being prepared for multi-careers

● developing a life-time career plan

● using training as a principal factor in career choice.

Work can be seen as a vehicle for:

● earning money for a roof over our heads and food in our belly

● earning money for luxuries

- self-expression

- new challenges

- meeting people

- developing skills

- continuous learning

- providing structure

- improving self-esteem

- a sense of belonging.

Re-learning

As a working woman, you do not have to be all things to all people. It is hard to unlearn the habits of a lifetime. You learnt at your mother's knee. You were taught in schools which were required to present certain values and beliefs. You wanted the approval of your father, so you behaved as you thought you should do, in order to gain that approval. When we are approved of, we are accepted and there is a sense of belonging. When we are fed this sense of belonging, we can survive. There is someone to look after us. A sense of belonging is a natural part of our survival system. However, women tend to think they must be supported (food, shelter, financially) in order to exist. Throughout history this has been so. Men have been the hunters and providers, while women have remained behind to tend the home and children. Now the roles are changing, causing concern and an identity crisis for both sexes.

You have a choice. Maybe this doesn't make it any easier. Women don't have to be the primary carer. Women can work. Women can re-train. Women can choose – if they allow themselves to.

Overcoming fear and guilt

Most women condition themselves to expect marriage, babies and maybe a little job. Women tend to believe that their needs and wants come last – after the partner, the family, the house and anything else. However, if we can overcome the guilt of enjoying success and power and if we can support ourselves through the fear of self-expression, we can find further fulfilment at work and in business.

A holistic approach

Work is only one part of our life. We also have friends, lovers, children, parents, hobbies, health and fitness, daydreaming and sleep. When we look at work, it is not only about money. It is about personal development, learning, challenge and using our skills and knowledge to make a contribution. A **holistic approach** to work means to take all of ourselves, mind, body and spirit, into account when planning our career.

PROMOTING SKILLS AND STRENGTHS

Most people undervalue their skills, strengths and experience. Women especially tend to undersell themselves. There is a buzz phrase in the workplace – **transferable skills**. This means looking at your skills, strengths and experience across the board and applying them to different areas of your life. For example, organising social events could be transferred to becoming a conference organiser.

When we explore and categorise our skills, strengths and experiences, we not only gain a toolbox to work from, but more importantly, we gain confidence and confirmation that we are worthwhile and useful.

Emerging from the shell

It may be traditionally female to be modest, shy and retiring. But we also have a need to be noticed, appreciated and to use and develop our skills and strengths. When we define ourselves, we feel in control and powerful. There is no shame in coming out of the shell into the limelight. We all deserve a little praise.

Accepting the positive

When we own our **positive qualities**, we are affirming ourselves and the importance of our experience. When we tell other people of our positive qualities, we are defining ourselves – not allowing someone else to do it for us. There is nothing helpful about promoting our negative so that other people won't feel insecure.

Being open to change

Taking a risk is frightening. Changing the way you think and behave can be threatening, not only to you, but to those around you. But if you don't open yourself up – you'll never know just how good you really are, will you?

If you are working, how do you see yourself at work? If you are preparing to return to work, how would you like to see yourself? Using word, shapes and colour, describe your image of yourself. You could describe how you see yourself right now or maybe how you would like to be seen by others.

Fig. 6. How I see myself at work.

COMPILING A SELF-INVENTORY

My strengths

What personal qualities do you have (across the board, not just in a work situation) *eg* integrity, honesty, a sense of humour?

My work values and motivations

This exercise looks at your personal needs for work. Tick those which you would regard as important.

a large business	fast pace	regular hours
a small business	financial security	respect from others
accomplishment	gaining knowledge	routine
activity	having authority	self-development
attention to detail	having feedback	self-respect
autonomy	having responsibility	sense of community
being a team member	having support	sense of purpose
being appreciated	helping society	social interaction
being efficient	identity	status
being expert	in the country	stress
being of service	independence	supervising others
being precise	influence	taking risks
being pro-active	irregular hours	time freedom
being supervised	loyalty	to be a success
belonging	making decisions	to be indoors
change	meeting deadlines	to be outdoors
close to home	mostly sitting	to motivate
communication	mostly standing	to support others
competitiveness	organising	tranquillity
contentment	overcoming challenges	travel
creativity	overtime	usefulness
developing new skills	perks	using existing skills
discipline	pleasing others	using lots of energy
dressing casually	pressure	using my intellect
dressing well	promotion	wisdom
earning commission	public contact	working alone
excitement	recognition	working with others

Checklist

1. Check out the similarities which exist between you and your mother. Do you share similar attitudes about work and money?

2. What are your beliefs about work, women, marriage, money and men?

3. How much time do you spend being or doing something without really being aware of why?

4. How has the way you were brought up affected your expectations as a working adult?

5. Do you believe you are a "typical" woman?

6. What makes you fearful about developing your potential at work?

7. How do you express your male side? Should you be more "male" at work?

8. How does risking change make you feel?

9. What really makes you tick at this moment in time?

10. What do you need in your working life right now? Do you want to work? If you received a cheque for £1,000 every week for the rest of your life, would you want to work?

CASE STUDIES

Maria is caught in the middle

Maria's mother has a restrained sense of ambition. She has worked as a secretary for the same company for 20 years and although she has been promoted, she hasn't pushed herself forward as much as she would have liked to. Her husband is self-employed and sees his wife's skills as being complementary to his business. Maria's older sister has broken free and works abroad and Maria is left with a sense that she should follow her mother into a safe job where her talents should be used to support another.

Carol is out on her own

Carol's mother saw her life's work as the family, especially since her husband died when Carol was quite young. Carol left home early and married in her 20s. She is strongly driven to achieve and pull her roots out of what she sees as her family's doldrums. However, she has no parental role model to follow with regard to work and so has to seek out and learn for herself.

Diane has a secret

Diane's children are high achievers and she has learnt from them that there are opportunities out there. She is unconsciously held back by her friends, who are afraid to lose her. Diane secretly admires strong businesswomen but lacks the confidence to develop her skills and so believes that she can never be successful.

DISCUSSION POINTS

1. How has the role of working women changed from your mother's generation to your own?

2. Why are there more job opportunities for women now? What traditionally male-dominated work areas would you consider exploring and why?

3. Which female qualities could work well in the workplace and why? Choose two businesswomen whom you admire and analyse how they use their qualities.

3
The Empowered Woman

DEFINING POWER

What does the word 'power' mean to you? Which of the following fits your image of the word?

money	father	politics
control	manipulation	men
aggression	dominance	big
magic	sex	authority
mother	status	strong
secret	knowledge	overwhelming
benevolent	God	

Are there any other words or images you associate with the word 'power'?

The power of choice

Most people tend to have negative images of power. We are frightened by the concept. In reality, we are all powerful. We have physical, emotional, mental and spiritual power. We have the **power of choice**. You have the power to put down this book. You have the power to allow the contents of this book to challenge you – if you choose.

Power is about choice. Some people say, money equates to power. But money itself is an inanimate object, it is what people do with money that gives it power. A knife can be used to create a delicious and nutritious meal or it can be used to stab someone. We each have a mind and a body. It is our choice what we do with both. We have the power to decide. If you had a box of chocolates and didn't like coffee creams, you would use your power of choice not to eat them. Life is similar. We have choices.

Some decisions are forced upon us by external circumstances such as redundancy and we seem to have little choice. But we do have a choice of internal response – we can view the enforced decision negatively or positively. We can see the situation with resentment, offering little opportunity, thereby not taking advantage of it. Or we can see the decision as an opportunity for a positive experience.

Sometimes we find ourselves in a rut and we make a conscious decision that something has to change. We instigate the change. We choose. But somewhere along the line, it all gets a bit risky. Things aren't quite as easy as we had thought. It starts to frighten us. We can experience the fear and the uncertainty and accept it as a natural part of our nature and still move forward.

Or we may be so paralysed by fear and the threat that we may be successful, that we may fund fulfilment, that we never risk change. We never express our power. We have still made a choice, but it is a choice to hide away. To stay stuck. Better the devil we know.

The empowered woman

The empowered woman is someone who demonstrates the following qualities:

● efficient perception of reality

● acceptance of self and others

● spontaneity and naturalness

● creativity

● ability to love and be loved

● ability to laugh, play and have fun

● forgiveness and compassion for self and others

● a sense of philosophical humour

● discrimination between means and ends

● autonomy

● ability to set boundaries and limits appropriately

● ability to make healthy choices

- a problem-centred approach

- a connection with spiritual experience.

Empowerment comes from within. It is the result of accessing inner resources and externalising them. The working woman is a powerful being who can balance, change and make a valuable contribution to business.

Exercise

1. Give examples of being powerless and describe your feelings from being powerless.

2. Gives examples of being powerful and describe your feelings from being powerful.

DEVELOPING THE RIGHT BEHAVIOUR

Using appropriate verbal and non-verbal styles helps to give the right impression at work and in business. Experts say that appearance and body language accounts for almost everything during the first few moments of meeting someone. In order to feel and convey an impression of positive power, we need to develop assertive skills and behaviour.

Verbal and non-verbal behaviours

Assertive behaviour

smiling	proximity
relaxed tone of voice	clear voice
sounding sincere	being in control
fluent	emphasising key words
relaxed jaw	being firm
being direct	brief statements
problem-solving	using questions
criticising constructively	sharing

Passive behaviour

excessive apologies	hedging *eg* perhaps
disclaimers *eg* I'm probably wrong but –	fillers *eg* um, well, y'know

powerless voice
tag questions *eg* aren't I right?
allowing the invasion of personal space
meek tone of voice
talking little
whining
being hesitant
throat swallowing
ghost smile
fiddling
covering mouth with hand
rambling

self-effacing remarks
avoiding eye contact
handwashing
allowing interruptions
talking quietly
speaking in a monotone
speaking jerkily
licking lips
being evasive
shuffling feet
stepping back

Aggressive/controlling behaviour

harsh tone of voice
staring eyes
talking loudly
ignoring responses
using sarcasm
abrupt tone
striding round
threatening questions
using put downs
being opinionated

set mouth
interrupting
talking quickly
stabbing fingers
shouting
fist thumping
crossing arms
using 'shoulds and oughts'
being boastful
ignoring other people's
  feelings

Exercise

1. Which assertive, aggressive and passive behaviours do you
    exhibit?

2. Without showing your responses, ask two friends which behaviours
    they think you show.

BECOMING MORE CONFIDENT

Confidence is a mixture of emotional and mental states; pride, self-respect, positive self-talk, empowerment plus assertive behaviour.

Positive self-talk

'I can do this' is so much more positive that 'I can't do this'. You may feel frightened or apprehensive but you can still have a go. When we define positive self-talk, this doesn't mean not acknowledging the anxious feelings. Rather than saying 'I'm scared witless about this job interview. I'm no good and no one will like me', we can admit our fear while at the same time telling ourselves 'It's OK to feel anxious, but I am going to do the best I can at this interview'.

Exercise

1. Write down six negative things you say to yourself.

2. Write down six positive statements to counterbalance the above.

3. Write down six 'things I find difficult to be confident about' (*eg* going to the dentist, standing up to my family, selling an idea to a publisher).

4. Write down six 'things I find easy to be confident about' (*eg* my communication skills, I can cook a good cheese and potato pie).

Taking risks

The only way to change is to **take risks**. But taking risks is scary and unpredictable. What if the change doesn't work? So what. You are allowed to make mistakes. You can handle looking silly for a moment. We might risk a change of career, returning to work after having children, re-training or stepping up into management.

Exercise

1. How might you take a risk at work?

2. What would you like to happen from taking this risk?

3. What do you fear happening from taking this risk?

4. How likely is it to really happen?

Approval seeking

When we have a need for approval, we may become a people-pleaser, fear criticism, fear failure, feel unworthy and ignore our own needs. The need for approval can hold us back from developing ourselves in a work situation.

Exercise

1. Which behaviours do you have which may indicate you seek approval from others? (*eg* asking if they mind, worrying over how you are being received.)

2. Identify and explain what you feel is being threatened by your need for approval. (*eg* if I'm not approved of I won't be needed.)

Self-esteem

A healthy sense of **self-esteem** is central to the empowered woman. Possible reasons for low self-esteem:

*   childhood loss of a parent through divorce or death, resulting in insecurity

*   overly critical parents resulting in self-criticism and feelings of inferiority

*   parental overindulgence resulting in an unwillingness to take personal responsibility

*   parental neglect resulting in feelings of worthlessness

*   parental overprotectiveness resulting in distrust

*   parental rejection resulting in self-rejection.

To feel loved and accepted when young, we tried hard to please and be perfect. Sometimes it seemed the harder we tried to please the big people, the less it worked. As a result, we may have withheld our efforts, fearing to make a mistake. As we grew into adulthood, we may have developed strong feelings of responsibility when things went wrong and a reluctance to accept credit when something went right. Low self-esteem can lead to a fear of failure and rejection, isolation, perfectionism and a negative self-image. All of these feelings can make us avoid taking risks in a work situation.

Exercise

1. Which of your behaviours indicate you have low self-esteem (*eg* rushing round trying to be good at everything)?

2.   Identify what you feel is being hurt by your low self-esteem (*eg* not being good enough).

When we begin to see our skills more realistically, our self-esteem increases. We interact with others more confidently and value our strengths as well as our limitations. We become more willing to take risks and recognise that we can learn from our mistakes.

OVERCOMING FEAR

The experience of fear as an emotional and mental state can be so overwhelming that we go out of our way to avoid experiencing it. We avoid situations which evoke this powerful emotion because we believe that we can't handle the feeling or what is causing the feeling.

Fears that happen to us
Certain things happen to us which are outside of our control such as age, illness, loss of financial security, redundancy or retirement.

Fears which involve our instigation
There are certain events which we can make happen such as returning to study, a career change, being interviewed or using the telephone.

If we choose to let fear paralyse us, we experience additional feelings of helplessness and powerlessness. We feel little, exposed, vulnerable – like a child again.

However, fear is a natural state. We can still feel powerful when feeling fearful. The power comes from accepting the fear while at the same time doing what is causing the fear, because doing something makes us feel in control and powerful. When a child shrinks with fear and becomes helpless, the parent will take the child's hand, reassure it, talk to it gently and with compassion and encourage it to move forward. In essence, this is what we need to do when we experience fear. It is as if the part that is encouraging and reassuring (our nurturing, parent-like self) needs to take the hand of our fearful side (our child-like self). We need to be our own loving parent.

TAKING RESPONSIBILITY FOR OURSELVES

Some women tend to have an overdeveloped sense of **responsibility**. We may have grown up believing that we were responsible for the way our parents felt and behaved. As a result, we may assume responsibility for the feelings and needs of others today, even in a work situation. This could result in being a perfectionist or a high achiever.

When we accept that we are not responsible for the actions or feelings of others, we can begin to take care of ourselves and delegate responsibility more. When we can nurture and support ourselves, we are better equipped to help others. But we shouldn't help others in place of ourselves.

Using the 'I' statement

The 'I' statement is a reflection of ownership. When we use it, the word indicates we are owning our thoughts, feelings and behaviours. Instead of saying, 'you make me angry', and blaming others, we say, 'I feel angry about what you have just said', and own our feelings.

Nurturing our inner child

The inner child is part of our mental and emotional make-up. It is made up of recordings of our early years representing feelings, responses, experiences and old behaviour. There are two sides to the inner child, the adopted and the free (see Figure 7). The adopted side represents the negative experiences and pain of our childhood and the automatic responses we have stored within our psyche. These responses can emerge in adulthood if we feel threatened or hurt. Our free inner child is our innocence, our spontaneity and magical creativity – it is part of our true essence.

We can be in a work situation and experience adopted or free inner child reactions and behaviours.

Becoming our own parent

The inner parent is part of our mental and emotional make-up (see Figure 8). It represents attitudes and behaviour learnt from external sources, especially our parents. Whether or not we are parents ourselves, these qualities can emerge under 'parental-type' conditions.

One of the more significant roles women tend to take on is that of carer. When we were growing up, it is possible that we had to take care of others (siblings or parents), meaning that we didn't have time to form our own identity. Taking care of others can make us feel indispensable and needed. As a result, we may tend to rescue others (even choosing a rescuing type of career), ignore our own needs and feel inadequate. We can be in a work situation and experience negative or positive inner parent reactions and behaviours.

Negative (adopted)	Positive (free)
powerless	innocent
helpless	fun loving
demanding	curious
abandoned	imaginative
victim	spontaneous
lonely	magical
hurt	energetic
vulnerable	open
rejected	loved
dependent	curious
whining	exuberant
fidgeting	excited

Fig. 7. Characteristics of the inner child.

Negative	Positive
overprotective	direct
smothering	loving
controlling	nurturing
critical	unconditional
manipulative	encouraging
demanding	protective
conditional	supportive
unloving	sharing
authoritarian	responsible
moralistic	listener
accusing	caring

Fig. 8. Characteristics of the inner parent.

Checklist

1. If you are frightened of your own power, this makes you afraid of yourself.

2. Are you frightened to take charge? Are you frightened of getting what you want?

3. If you want to become more assertive, enrol on an adult education class.

4. In order to become more positive, you need to tune into your mental chatterbox and change the negative tapes to positive ones.

5. What is so bad about taking a risk and making a mistake? Afraid to look silly? Scared you won't cope?

6. Do you still seek approval from mummy and daddy? Have you transferred this need for approval to your partner or those you work with?

7. Think of your good points with pride.

8. You can either accept or change your bad points.

9. Make friends with fear by understanding and working with it.

10. Taking responsibility for your thoughts, feelings and actions means you are one powerful lady.

11. Learn to like, respect, and if possible, love yourself as the nice person you are – warts and all.

CASE STUDIES

Maria is frustrated

Maria is dynamic and fun but tends to come across somewhat aggressively. Deep down she wants to be a career woman but is afraid of commitment and the threat of success. Her mother brings home an income which supplements her husband's business and Maria is faintly scornful of what she perceives as her mother's lack of ambition. She experiences her father as being distant, successful and always busy. There is an unspoken expectation by her parents, that Maria will 'settle down to a good job soon'. Maria wants to be approved of by her father as a businesswoman but unconsciously she is emulating her mother by holding herself back. She believes that, by appearing busy and being aggressive, she is achieving a positive image.

Carol begins networking

Having made a major career change, Carol now has to start at the bottom. Coming from management in one area of business to the lower rungs of another has left her feeling powerless and anxious about not being in control. To compensate for these feelings, she volunteers for several courses in order to learn and network, so that she can begin to get to know the company and other people.

Diane breaks out

Diane is ready for some kind of career change now. One son is at university and the other is still living at home and working as a computer programmer. Her role as parent is dwindling and she has only ever worked for one company. Her skills are limited as is her confidence, but she strongly feels this is her time to 'break out'.

DISCUSSION POINTS

1. How do you interpret and use your power within a working environment? How can personal power be destructive to the self?

2. Define how your female qualities express themselves and how your inner male gives those qualities expression and form.

3. What is authority? Choose a male and a female role model in business and define the skills and qualities they demonstrate. Analyse your likes and dislikes.

4
Developing the Right Skills

This section is all about the analysis of your skills and whether you want to use them or learn new ones.

IDENTIFYING JOB-SPECIFIC SKILLS

If you haven't worked for some time, the initial analysis may refer to **unpaid work** such as bringing up a family, working in the home, helping friends, hobbies or doing voluntary work.

Paid work may be defined as part or full-time.

Exercise

Figure 9 shows a list of job-types which describe paid or unpaid work.

1. On a sheet of paper, head two columns 'Paid Work' and 'Unpaid Work'. Go through the list, placing the job-types in the two columns. Ignore the job-types you have not experienced. Remember that paid work is work that you have done part or full-time for money. Unpaid work is something you have done for fun, to help someone out, around the home or for the family.

2. On a second sheet of paper, head two columns 'Would like to learn' and 'Would like to increase skills'. In the first column, place the job-types you have a yen to learn and explore and in the second column, the job-types you have some experience of and would like to expand upon. There will be certain job-types that have no appeal – leave them out.

ANALYSING YOUR SKILLS

You may not be aware that the skills you use on a day-to-day or occasional basis can be transferred to all kinds of jobs. Go through the skills listed on page 51 and circle those you use around the home.

accounting	construction	forensic science	meteorology
acting	consumer	forestry	mining
acupuncturist	protection	fund-raising	museum work
administration	conservation	furniture	musician
advertising	contract mngt.	restoration	natural science
agriculture	copywriting	gourmet cooking	nursing
ambulance driver	corporate planning	graphic designer	occupational
animal training	counselling	groom	therapy
antiques	courier	growing fruit/veg	office work
archaeology	court work	hairdressing	optician
architecture	craft projects	herbalism	organise
archive work	creating clothes	holiday guide	trips/events
armed forces	customs work	homeopath	osteopath
aromatherapy	dancing	horticulture	painting/
art and design	demolition work	hotel work	decorating
art evaluation	dentistry	house repairs	personnel
assembling things	designing	house restoration	pharmacology
auctioneering	jewellery	hydrography	pharmacy
author	diagnostics	hydrology	photography
banking	dietician	industrial relations	physiotherapy
beautician	diplomatic work	information	picture framing
bookbinding	director	provider	piloting
book-keeping	display work	insurance	planning routes
breeding animals	dog handler	interior design	play group work
brewer	drama coach	inventing	playwright
broadcasting	drawing plans	investment mngt.	plumbing
building society	dressmaker	journalism	police work
building work	driving instructor	lab technician	politics
career guidance	economic analysis	landscape gdng.	printing
caring for animals	editor	lecturing	prison service
carpentry	education	legal services	probation
cartography	electrics	librarianship	production mngt.
catering	electronics	machine operation	project engineer
childcare	engineering	machine	property dev.
chiropodist	environmental	supervisions	public relations
chiropractic	health	management	public
church work	factory inspector	mngt. consultancy	spokesperson
cleaning	farming	marketing	publishing
clerical	fashion modelling	market research	quality control
clinical	film direction	massage	quantity surveying
psychology	finance	mechanical repairs	radiography
coaching a sport	consultancy	mechanics	recreation mngt.
coastguard	fisheries work	medical	reflexology
community work	flight operations	administration	repairing
composing music	floral design	merchant banking	research
computer work	food preparation	metallurgy	research scientist

Fig. 9. Job-types.

50

restoring textile items	silversmith	surgeon	transport mngt.
	singer	surveying	typography
retail management	site engineer	systems	undertaker
riding instructor	social sciences	tax work	upholsterer
secretary	social services	taxi driver	vehicle mntnance
security	solving crime	technical writing	vet
selling	speech therapy	telephone work	waitress
servicing	sport	town planning	woodworker
shiatsu	statistics	training	youth worker
shipping	stockbroking	traffic operations	
sign writer	storage/delivery	translator	

1. growing plants – landscape gardening – garden maintenance – growing vegetables/fruit

2. caring for animals – pet grooming – pet training – caring for ill pets

3. repairing electrical appliances – interior design – painting – wallpapering – repairing furniture – plumbing – replacing flooring – organising utilities/tradespeople – making soft furnishings

4. sewing – co-ordinating clothes – care of clothing – creating or remodelling clothing – repairing clothing – assisting others with personal care – giving haircuts

5. providing first aid – organising a medicine cabinet – home nursing – caring for special needs

6. planning menus – gourmet cooking – entertaining – food preparation for the family – organising recreational activities

7. evaluation and purchase of food, appliances, furnishings etc – managing household expenses – handling credit/loan applications – budgeting – using a home computer

8. managing your time – setting priorities – supervising others – motivating others – supporting in crisis – finding sources of information – counselling – tutoring children

9. driving – route planning – making routine vehicle repairs – booking accommodation

10. cleaning windows – safety in the home – hygiene in food preparation – laundry – carpet and upholstery cleaning – housekeeping.

Transferring general skills to jobs

Which of the above skills would you like to earn a living by?

To which kinds of jobs could those skills be transferred across to?

Exercise

Below is a list of skills.

1. On a sheet of paper, head two columns 'Can do well' and 'Haven't tried'. Go through the list, placing the skills in the two columns.

2. On a second sheet of paper, head two columns 'Would like to learn' and 'Would like to increase skills'. In the first column, place the skills you have a yen to learn and explore and in the second column, the skills you have some experience of and would like to expand upon. There will be certain skills that have no appeal – leave them out.

Skills analysis

administration	improvising	researching
assembling things	keyboarding	selling
clerical	leading	tending animals
computing	making things	using machines
designing	managing money	working with
diagnosing	organising	colour and images
dissecting information	performing	working with
driving	problem-solving	figures
growing things	promoting change	working with music
helping others	repairing	working with words

ANALYSING TASKS AND SKILLS

To further define our skills, we can take a job, break it down into tasks and then break the tasks down into skills.

Job: Shop owner

Tasks	**Skills**
ordering stock	dealing with reps
stock control	organisation
selling	persuasiveness, knowing what is wanted
staff management	disciplinary procedures, tact
publicity	design, literacy
book-keeping/accounts	numeracy

This is useful to do for the following reasons:

- to remind us that we do have skills
- to identify transferable skills
- for information to put on a CV
- for information to use at an interview.

Exercise

On a piece of paper, head first column 'Tasks' and the second 'Skills'. Take one job you have had in your working life and list in the 'Tasks' column all the relevant tasks associated with that job. In the 'Skills' column, write down all the skills you used in that task.

IDENTIFYING PERSONAL DEVELOPMENT SKILLS

Below is a list of personal characteristics; underline the ones that you most identify with.

adaptable	consistent	imaginative	people-pleaser
adventurous	daring	independent	perfectionist
aggressive	decisive	innovative	persistent
aloof	dependable	intellectual	positive
ambitious	easy-going	introspective	reliable
assertive	efficient	just	reserved
capable	emotional	loyal	resilient
caring	energetic	methodical	resourceful
cautious	exciteable	objective	security-minded
changeable	forceful	obstinate	self-reliant
cheerful	gentle	open-minded	sensitive to others
co-operative	hard-working	organised	stable
competitive	helpful	outgoing	tactful
confident	humorous	passive	trustworthy

The nature of our personal characteristics can be used:

- to clarify our work values and motivations for when we want to return to work or change career direction

- for self-awareness

- to build confidence.

Exercise

Ask one person who knows you well and one person who knows you

	Angry	Submissive	Confident
Voice tone/pitch	loud, harsh, clipped	monotonic, mumbling	clear, controlled, well-paced
Facial expressions	glaring, set, red/white face	looking away, nervous smile	direct eye contact, head up
Posture	closed body, invasive	withdrawn, hugging self	upright, open, fairly still
Gestures	fist thumping, arms waving	fiddling, tapping, twitching	expansive hand movements
Language used	'you'd better', 'I'm telling you'	'I'm awfully sorry', 'would you mind'	'let's talk', 'how can we resolve this?'

Fig. 10. Giving yourself away.

casually to describe how they see you. Do other people give you the same personal characteristics as you give yourself?

Verbal and non-verbal communication skills

When we communicate, most of our messages are sent through the language of our body. How we sit, stand, use gestures and eye contact convey our unspoken thoughts and feelings to others.

Because we are often unaware of our **body language**, we can be saying one thing while our body language is indicating something else. Others will respond to the total picture of our communication, verbal and non-verbal, and if there are mixed messages we may not get the response we are looking for.

Customer care is a growing part of business. Whether it is answering the telephone, writing letters or having direct contact with clients or customers, more emphasis is being placed on communication skills. Every business is involved in customer care.

Figure 10 gives an overview of verbal and non-verbal language used to indicate three specific emotional states.

Listen to the words you use,
be careful how you pick and choose.
How you stand and what you say
creates an image that lasts the day.

Your posture as you sit and stand
reflects your thought, your sleight of hand.
See eye to eye, a smile or two
leave an image that's good and true.

Our bodies speak in ways untold,
a hint, a spark, a message bold.
If you want to win the game
make body and speech resound the same.

Using questions

Questions are used to clarify our understanding and move us forward. We use questions all the time in business:

- dealing with customer's queries

- dealing with staff

● interviewing others

● when learning something new.

There are a number of ways in which to ask a question:

● *Closed*: questions which elicit a yes or a no, *eg* 'Have you got Mr Smith's file?'

● *Open*: questions which elicit a more in-depth response, *eg* 'What qualities do you think you can bring to this job?'

● *Probing*: questions which can develop responses, *eg* 'What makes you think Jean is being aggressive towards you?'

● *Affective*: questions which relate to underlying feelings, *eg* 'How does this make you feel about the job?'

Being able to ask the right question, using the most helpful format, is useful. We feel more in control when we ask – we understand and therefore develop our knowledge.

Listening skills

Most of us can hear – but do we really **listen**? When we are very emotional, we don't listen very well, we are full of our own thoughts and feelings, eager to get our say in. If what we are hearing doesn't correspond to our views, we tend to withdraw or over-ride our listening skills.

Quality listening skills involve:

● observing body language and voice tone

● listening to ourselves as well as others

● self-discipline

● making others feel safe and accepted.

What stops effective listening?

What kind of physical and emotional barriers can interfere with listening?

Exercise
Sit down with someone you know well and talk for five minutes on any subject with your eyes closed (your partner's eyes are open). Then reverse the situation, you have your eyes open and your partner's are shut. Observe and discuss your thoughts and feelings.

Further communication skills

● Giving instructions or coaching others.

● Communicating information to our subordinates, peers or superiors.

● Written communications skills via report writing, memos and letters.

● Telephone skills via customer care, sales, professionals or internal communication.

Leadership skills

A leader is self-sufficient and can help others without giving their own power away. A woman can blend together her feminine qualities of intuition and compassion with the inner male qualities of leadership and facilitation. Positive leadership qualities include:

using common sense	facilitating other people's
courtesy	development
being positive	valuing the efforts of others
expressing your individuality	listening to others
obtaining results from people	being committed
taking responsibility	taking risks
looking calm	providing motivational energy
being human	never giving up
challenging yourself	fairness
approachability	praising others
creativity	admitting mistakes
planning with others	providing focus
knowing your job	knowing your people
decisiveness	confronting problems
enthusiasm	empowering others
inspiring others	projecting into the future
treating others as real people	

Do you:

- ask questions

- lead and direct others

- convey to people that you care about them

- draw people out

- take the initiative in relationships

- talk things through with people

- help others to develop and learn

- give credit to others

- show appreciation

- show sensitivity to others' feelings

- pay attention to what people want?

Presentation skills

If you are, or have aspirations to be, a manager, trainer or self-employed, you are going to be involved in giving presentations. This involves the successful synthesis of a number of factors – appearance, knowing your subject, preparation, delivery and handling the audience.

Some hints

- empty pockets

- button up jacket

- avoid fussy detail

- don't hold hands behind back or fold arms

- keep body open

- use hand movements with palms up

- avoid pointing fingers

- smile occasionally

- make eye contact

- end statements in a low tone

- draw attention to the face

- wear stronger make-up than normal with special attention to lips and eyes

- for a formal presentation wear classic clothes, a dark navy suit, a simple blouse, bold but not distracting necklace and earrings

- for an informal presentation wear less severe clothes, maybe a lighter neutral jacket over a bolder dress

- practise reading out loud to improve pronunciation and pace

- practise deep breathing from the diaphragm.

USING PROFESSIONAL DEVELOPMENT SKILLS

These skills have been defined in this section as being problem-solving, decision-making and entrepreneurial.

Problem-solving

We use problem-solving abilities most of the time, but we are probably unaware of the processes involved, such as:

- taking ownership

- defining the situation through information gathering

- having realistic goals

- making realistic predictions

- monitoring the implementation of plan

- evaluation of plan.

Additional skills

- using positive self-talk

- having helpful beliefs

- having accurate perceptions of yourself

Decision-making
How do you make decisions?

- logically and objectively

- morally and ethically

- impulsively

- by delaying until the problem solves itself

- via feeling and intuition

- passively according to the expectations of others

- by getting too involved with detail and the assessment process.

Entrepreneurial
This is an overall skill which has the following components:

- the ability to be flexible

- being multi-skilled in order to diversify within a job, or to transfer skills or to run two or three careers together

- the ability to spot an opportunity

- the ability to create an opportunity

- the ability to develop an opportunity.

Checklist

1. If you want to assess your skills, take a psychometric test with a careers counsellor.

2. Your local adult education college will have several courses on personal development, body language and basic counselling skills.

3. If you are working, ask to go on a course to improve your telephone skills.

4. If you want to improve your business writing skills, enrol on an adult education class or if working, ask to go on a course.

5. To improve management skills, presentation skills or problem solving skills, enrol on an adult education class, if working ask to be put on a course or you can take a private course.

CASE STUDIES

Maria wants to be accepted

Maria has good job-specific skills related to her secretarial and administration experience. Although gregarious in her behaviour, her body language is often at odds with her verbal communication. She hasn't yet learnt to listen to herself – she often says what she believes others want to hear so that she will be accepted. Her communication style often comes across aggressively.

Carol transfers her skills

Carol has transferred her job-specific skills from catering to the Civil Service. As a homeowner and mother, she has also built up a considerable base of general skills. Several of the courses on offer at her place of work involve empowerment and personal development, so she is increasing her self-awareness all the time. Her job-specific skills are being developed on the job.

Diane wins on maturity

Diane has considerable general skill as a homeowner, mother and single parent. Her job-specific skills are limited. However, her maturity works for her, bringing many solid and positive personal qualities and strengths. The area she is weakest on is occupational knowledge and training opportunities and the self-belief she can go for it.

DISCUSSION POINTS

1. Which personal qualities might you (or other women) use in a leadership role?

2. How do you use your body at work to convey messages?

3. Define ways in which you might use entrepreneurial skills to develop your work.

5
Guidance in Occupations and Training

BREAKING AWAY FROM STEREOTYPES

Business tradition has been largely formed by men and male conditioning, and women have colluded with men in the acceptance of work roles and values.

Each gender has mental, emotional and physical **differences**. But each person, as an individual, expresses those differences in unique ways. A man can be compassionate, nurturing and intuitive while doing his work as a brickie. A woman can be decisive, active and logical while doing her work as a nurse.

Taking the idea further into occupational areas, we learn from school, the media and parental conditioning to expect certain career paths. It's OK for a man to have ambitions as a printer, entrepreneur or politician. It's OK for a woman to want to be a midwife, office worker or model. We live in a mainly patriarchal business world and women subtly support this ethos by not accepting responsibility for their qualities and contribution to a working culture. Now women want a wider choice of work. Because of the more female qualities of flexibility and adaptability, women are widening the choice for themselves. This may have a backlash as men see more women entering the workplace and taking the jobs. But both genders can develop and utilise flexibility in order to reskill themselves.

Traditional stereotype occupations may include the following:

Male

surgeon	plasterer	bank manager
dentist	pilot	bus driver
construction labourer	fire fighter	farmer
electrician	accountant	company director
brickie	chef	astronaut
architect	doctor	scientist
mechanic	programmer	politician
lawyer	betting shop manager	forest worker
investment analyst	scaffolder	train driver

63

| refuse collector | butcher | carpenter |
| plumber | stockbroker | |

Female

librarian	clerk	teacher
nurse	beautician	waitress
receptionist	shop assistant	secretary
childminder	housekeeper	health visitor
counsellor	dietician	hairdresser
home help	midwife	playgroup organiser
personnel officer	telephonist	window dresser
book-keeper	social worker	veterinary nurse
word processing	training	wages clerk
supervisor		

FINDING A JOB WITH A FUTURE

Certain sectors of industry and commerce are disappearing whilst growth areas are forming all the time. In order to stay in work, we need to be aware of which jobs have a future. We need to have our fingers on the pulse of current trends, so that we can develop the appropriate skills and gain the right kind of experience. Potential growth areas include:

● IT and technology

● training

● business services

● security and protective services

● health

● science

● the environment.

TRAINING ROUTES

Adult education

If you are unsure of a particular career direction, a ten week **evening class** or a one day **workshop** may help you to decide. Typical courses might include computing, counselling skills, word processing, cookery, vehicle maintenance, languages or designing stained glass.

Further education

You can be a full- or part-time student. A typical course might include accounting, archaeology, tourism or journalism. General education qualifications at GCSE, AS or A-levels, and vocational qualifications such as GNVQs and NVQs are available in a variety of subjects.

Higher education

If you are considering entering university but don't have the relevant qualifications or you feel unsure of your study skills, you could try an access course for a year. These are foundation courses for mature students or those without qualifications who want to enter higher education. You can choose an access course which complements the type of study you wish to enter, *eg* business studies. Upon successful completion, you may then be offered a university place. Access courses may be offered through your local further education college or university.

At university, you can study full or part-time or enrol on a sandwich course. Subjects may include degrees and diplomas in health, environmental studies, humanities, art, computing, engineering and business.

Open learning

Due to health problems or dependents, you may not be able to attend a college or university on a regular basis. Open learning is a flexible option for re-training. There are several institutes which offer learning using the post, telephone, video, radio, TV, and summer schools. Certificates, diplomas and degrees are available in a wide choice of subjects.

General education

GCSE

This stands for General Certificate of Secondary Education which replaces the former GCE O level and CSE examinations. It is the principal means of assessing the National Curriculum at Key Stage 4. Emphasis is placed on the candidates demonstrating what they know and can do. A further feature is coursework assignments.

GCE advanced supplementary (AS) level

These are designed to broaden the curriculum for A level students. They represent the same intellectual standard as A level but have about half the content of A levels, requiring less study and teaching.

Vocational qualifications

The way forward for the 18 plus student with the necessary general education behind them is the professional qualification route involving BTEC National Certificates and Diplomas, and National Vocation Qualifications (NVQs) and General NVQs (GNVQs).

College certificates and diplomas

Some colleges offer their own certificates and diplomas which are internally validated.

National certificates and diplomas

BTEC (Business and Technology Education Council) and SCOTVEC (Scottish Vocational Education Council) offer awards at three levels – First, National and Higher National. At each of the levels, the student may obtain a certificate (generally for part-time students) or a diploma.

NVQs/SVQs

These are the qualifications of the future. They are acceptable in this country and in Europe. There are five levels ranging from foundation through to degree level. They are employer led which means that all the criteria set out in each NVQ (or SVQ in Scotland) has been specifically endorsed by individual trade, occupational or professional body.

In order to acquire an NVQ, you are assessed through direct observation to provide evidence that you have the skills necessary to do the job. You are required to provide further evidence of your knowledge. You can take part of an NVQ or the whole of it, and the skills and knowledge are transferable between occupations.

National Vocational Qualifications are based on national standards as set down by the lead bodies representing industry and commerce, *eg* engineering or business services. They are obtained through work-place assessment. There are five levels of competence: Level 1 indicates competence in mainly routine occupational activities through to Level 5 which indicates a higher level of professional competence. Each NVQ is made up of a number of units of competence which in turn contain a series of elements, each of which is individually assessed.

LOOKING AT SPECIFIC JOB AREAS

The following section provides an overview of possible opportunities and job-types within:

- Information technology

- Leisure and communication

- Security and protective services

- Science, engineering and maintenance

- Training and education

- Health, social and personal care

- Business services

- Animals, plants and land.

There is further information on training routes through awarding bodies.

Opportunities in it

Information technology (IT) is a growth area. The world is becoming more automated. Sadly this can suggest that the machine is taking over some areas of work. However, someone has to press the button. Becoming familiar with **computers** and technology is advisable.

Typical job types

- systems analyst

- programmer

- word processor operator

- desk top publishing

- data processing

- service technician

- teleworker (someone who is employed to work from home using a computer, modem, fax and telephone)

- hardware designer.

Awarding bodies offering training
British Computer Society (BCS)
Information Technology Industry Training Organisation (ITITO)
London Chamber of Commerce and Industry (LCCI)
City and Guilds (C & G)
Pitman Examination Institute (PEI)
RSA Examinations Board (RSA)
Business and Technology Education Council (BTEC)
Scottish Vocational Education Council (SCOTVEC).

Questions to ask myself

- Do I like working with things?
- Do I enjoy working with detail?
- Am I logically minded?
- Am I a problem-solver?

Opportunities in training and education

Vocational training is becoming a mega-buck market. As requirements for job-specific skills increase, more trainers are needed. Another potential growth area is private tutoring which reflects the changes in standard education within schools.

Typical job types

- training officer (working for a company)

- freelance trainer (offering courses and workshops to a variety of organisations)

- teaching English as a foreign language

- education (private tutoring, educational psychologist, education guidance worker, education welfare worker, special educational needs)

- further education lecturer

- sports coaching.

Awarding bodies offering training
London Chamber of Commerce and Industry (LCCI)
Business and Technology Education Council (BTEC)
City and Guilds (C & G)
Pitman Examination Institute (PEI)
RSA Examinations Board (RSA)
Institute of Supervision and Management (ISM)
Scottish Vocational Education Council (SCOTVEC)
Institute of Personnel and Development (IPD).

Questions to ask myself

- Am I patient?
- Can I draw people out?
- Do I have specialist knowledge?
- Can I motivate others?

Opportunities in leisure and communication
The home leisure market is increasing as more people want to build their leisure around the home base. Also as more people have leisure time due to a change in working structure, they are looking for entertainment and something to occupy their time and mind.

Typical job-types

- travel and tourism (consultancy)

- film and TV (performing, camerawork, production, writing)

- music (performing, writing, technician)

- hotel work (management, receptionist, chef, housekeeping etc)

- freelance journalism.

Awarding bodies offering training
Travel and tourism: Business and Technology Education Council (BTEC)
City and Guilds (C & G)
ABTA National Training Board (ABTA-NTB)
RSA Examinations Board (RSA)

	Scottish Vocational Education Council (SCOTVEC)
Journalism:	RSA Examinations Board (RSA) Periodicals Training Council (PTC) Scottish Vocational Education Council (SCOTVEC)
Media techniques:	City and Guilds (C & G)
Hotel work:	Hotel and Catering Training Company (HCTC) Business and Technology Education Council (BTEC) City and Guilds (C & G) Hotel and Catering and Institutional Management Association (HCIMA) Scottish Vocational Education Council (SCOTVEC)
Drama:	Business and Technology Education Council (BTEC).

Questions to ask myself

- Am I creative?
- Am I interested in what people want?
- Do I like interacting with others?
- Do I like entertaining others?

Opportunities in health, social and personal care

As our awareness and practice of good healthcare increases, we are living longer and becoming an elderly nation. This is one reason why care of the elderly is a potential growth area. Because of the changing structure in work patterns, career guidance is becoming more widely used. Again because of shifting work trends, childcare, especially for working parents, is an area of potential growth.

According to the Medical Women's Federation, one third of UK doctors will be women by the year 2000. Women comprise around half of house officers and a third of senior registrars, yet less than a fifth of hospital consultants and just over a quarter of GP principals.

Typical job-types

- psychology and counselling

- social work (youth worker)

- health (nursing, dietician, chiropody, doctoring, optician, midwifery, occupational therapist)

- natural health (acupuncture, chiropractic, homeopathy, herbalism, osteopathy)

- beauty (therapist or consultant)

- probationer

- career guidance

- childcare (child psychology, nursery work)

- care of the elderly.

Awarding bodies offering training

Care:	City and Guilds (C & G)
	Business and Technology Education Council (BTEC)
	Scottish Vocational Education Council (SCOTVEC)
Health/social care:	City & Guilds (C & G)
	Business and Technology Education Council (BTEC)
	RSA Examinations Board (RSA)
Childcare:	City and Guilds (C & G)
	Business and Technology Education Council (BTEC)
	Scottish Vocational Education Council (SCOTVEC)
Probation work:	City and Guilds (C & G)
	Scottish Vocational Education Council (SCOTVEC)
	Central Council for Education and Training in Social Work (CCETSW)
Beauty:	City and Guilds (C & G)
	Confederation of International Beauty Therapy and Cosmetology (CIBTAC)
	Vocational Training Charitable Training (VTCT)
	Business and Technology Education Council (BTEC)

Scottish Vocational Education Council (SCOTVEC).

Questions to ask myself

● Can I convey warmth and caring to others?
● Can I show sensitivity to others' feelings?
● Have I got good listening skills?
● Do I want to help others?

Opportunities in security and protective services

Because of the change in our social structure, partly contributed to by unemployment, crime prevention and security is high on the agenda for most people.

Typical job-types

● prison officer

● fire fighter

● ambulance worker

● police officer

● security officer.

Awarding bodies offering training
City and Guilds (C & G)
Security Industry Training Organisation (SITO)
Scottish Vocational Education Council (SCOTVEC).

Questions to ask myself

● Am I physically fit?
● Do I stay calm in a crisis?
● Am I disciplined?
● Can I think on my feet?

Opportunities in business services

As more companies outsource their work, the opportunities for freelancing in business services is increasing.

Typical job-types

- insurance

- accountancy

- employment agency

- management

- languages (European)

- marketing and PR

- photography

- graphic design

- personal finance (investment analyst, commodity broker)

- business administration.

Awarding bodies offering training

Accountancy: Pitman Examination Institute (PEI)
RSA Examinations Board (RSA)
Business and Technology Education Council (BTEC)
Association of Accounting Technicians (AAT)
London Chamber of Commerce and Industry (LCCI)
City and Guilds (C & G)
Scottish Vocational Education Council
(SCOTVEC)

Business admin: Pitman Examination Institute (PEI)
RSA Examinations Board (RSA)
Business and Technology Education Council (BTEC)
London Chamber of Commerce and Industry
(LCCI)
City and Guilds (C & G)
Scottish Vocational Education Council
(SCOTVEC)

Insurance: RSA Examinations Board (RSA)
Insurance Industry Training Council (IITC)
Chartered Insurance Institute (CII)

	Scottish Vocational Education Council (SCOTVEC)
Management:	City and Guilds (C & G)
	Management Verification Consortium (MVC)
	Henley Management College (HMC)
	RSA Examinations Board (RSA)
	Institute of Supervision and Management (ISM)
	Institute of Management (IM)
	National Examination Board for Supervisory Management (NEBSM)
	Business and Technology Education Council (BTEC)
	Scottish Vocational Education Council (SCOTVEC)
Languages:	London Chamber of Commerce and Industry (LCCI)
	City and Guilds (C & G)
Graphic design:	Business and Technology Education Council (BTEC)
	Open University (OU)
	RSA Examinations Board (RSA)
	City and Guilds (C & G)
Photography:	City and Guilds (C & G)
	Photography and Photographic Processing Industry Training Organisation (PPPITO)
	Business and Technology Education Council (BTEC)
	Scottish Vocational Education Council (SCOTVEC).

Questions to ask myself

- Am I adaptable?
- Can I develop an idea?
- Do I like working with others?
- Am I organised?

Opportunities in science, engineering and maintenance

According to the Institute of Physics, the industry employs 47 per cent of women physicists while a further 37 per cent are employed in education.

The Women's Engineering Society say that undergraduate courses related to engineering are available on merit and a woman is unlikely to be the sole woman on the course.

Typical job-types

- engineer (aeronautical, chemical, civil, marine, mechanical, production, structural, telecommunications)

- chemist

- pharmacist

- scientist

- vehicle maintenance.

Awarding bodies offering training

Engineering: City and Guilds (C & G)
                          Aviation Training Association (ATA)
                          British Agricultural and Garden Machinery
                             Association Ltd (BAGMA)
                          Scottish Vocational Education Council
                             (SCOTVEC)
                          Engineering Training Authority (ENTRA)
                          Electricity Training Association (ETA)
                          Business and Technology Education Council (BTEC)
                          Engineering Construction Industry Training Board
                             (ECITB)
                          Marine and Engineering Training Authority
                             (M&ETA)
                          Telecommunications Vocational Standards Council
                             (TVSC)

Vehicle maintenance: Automotive Management and Development
                             (AMD)
                          The Institute of the Motor Industry (IMI)
                          Motor Industry Training Standards Council
                             (MITSC)
                          Scottish Vocational Education Council
                             (SCOTVEC)
                          City and Guilds (C & G)

	Business and Technology Education Council (BTEC)
	Bus and Coach Training Ltd (BCT)
Science:	Business and Technology Education Council (BTEC)
	City and Guilds (C & G)
Pharmacy:	Chemical Industries Association (CIA)
	Association of the British Pharmaceutical Industry (ABPI)
	Business and Technology Education Council (BTEC)
	City and Guilds (C & G)
	Scottish Vocational Education Council (SCOTVEC).

Questions to ask myself

- Do I like finding out how things work?
- Am I good at dissecting information?
- Have I got manual dexterity?
- Can I research and classify?

Opportunities with animals, plants and land
According to London Women and Manual Trades:

- in advanced market economies, there is increasing interest on the part of government, training agencies and women's groups in women working in construction

- segregation is breaking down at professional level

- women account for around 11 per cent of the construction industry labour force (Department of Employment 1993) with around 86 per cent of them in clerical and administration jobs. Around 54 per cent of the construction labour force are craft and related workers but less than 1 per cent of these are female.

Typical job-types

- environment work (countryside ranger, forestry work, conservation officer, health officer, horticulture)

- planning work (town planning, architecture, surveying, conveyancing)

- manual trades (bricklayer, carpet fitter, carpenter, tiling, floorcovering, roofing, glazing, steeplejacking, plastering, joinery, painting and decorating, masonry)

- animal care.

Awarding bodies offering training

Land care: City and Guilds (C & G)
Business and Technology Education Council (BTEC)
National Examining Board for Agriculture, Horticulture and Allied Industries (NEBAHAI)
Scottish Vocational Education Council (SCOTVEC)
Industry Lead Body for Amenity Horticulture (ILBAH)

Animal care: City and Guilds (C & G)
National Examining Board for Agriculture, Horticulture and Allied Industries (NEBAHAI)
Animal Care Industry Lead Body (ACILB)
Scottish Vocational Education Council (SCOTVEC)
Sea Fish Industry Authority (SFIA)

Manual trades: City and Guilds (C & G)
Construction Industry Training Board (CITB)
Scottish Vocational Education Council (SCOTVEC)
Business and Technology Education Council (BTEC)
RSA Examinations Board (RSA)
Chartered Institute of Building (CIOB)
Electricity Training Association (ETA)
Glass Training Ltd (GTL)
Heating and Ventilation Contractors Association (HVCA)
Refrigeration Industry Board (RIB)
Heating and Ventilating Domestic Engineers National Joint Industry Council (HVDENJIC)

British Gas Plc (BG)
National Association of Plumbing, Heating and
Mechanical Services (NAPHMS).

Questions to ask myself

- Do I like working with my hands?
- Do I want to work outside?
- Do I like repairing things?
- Do I like animals?

THE NEXT STEP

For further sources of **occupational** information, contact or visit:

- your local careers office

- the library.

For further sources of **training** information, contact or visit:

- your local further education college

- your local adult education centre

- universities

- Training Access Points (TAPS)

- the library

- the awarding body.

For sources on **funding** for training, explore:

- career development loans

- adult bursaries (information from your local careers office)

- government schemes (your local job centre).

Checklist

1. For further information on any occupation, contact your local college, university or the awarding body.

2. For information on funding, contact your local TEC or the careers advice service. If you are claiming benefit, contact your local Jobcentre.

CASE STUDIES

Maria returns to college

Although Maria likes to think she is independent, she comes across as aggressive and defensive. She firmly believes in 'the new woman' but nevertheless finds it difficult to stand up for herself without putting down someone else in order to do it. As she becomes more aware of herself, she has decided to take a course in assertiveness. Her secretarial and administration work has put her firmly in touch with technology and computers and she has good skills in this direction, but she would like more challenge now and would consider serious training in order for a more committed and rewarding career. She is considering the idea of media studies after a temping assignment in an advertising agency.

Carol takes the NVQ route

Carol now works for a committed equal opportunities employer and has to develop strong personal qualities to move up the ladder. NVQs are currently being offered to staff and she has decided to take up the option.

Diane finds a key to training

During her time working for a printing company, Diane has had casual experience working on compugraphic machinery. This has sparked off an interest in using computers for design and layout.

DISCUSSION POINTS

1. How has your field of expertise or work been stereotyped?

2. What are the benefits of on-the-job learning?

3. How might you develop into a job with a future?

6
Leading the Way to the Top

INCORPORATING FEMALE QUALITIES IN BUSINESS

The successful businesswoman is **balanced**. She blends the female and male within to produce a holistic base from which to function. She actively cares about her own development, respects her colleagues' rights, facilitates her employees' development and recognises the intrinsic place of every business as a cog within the larger wheel of society.

The ideal qualities of a successful businesswoman may include:

- intuition
- logic
- compassion
- independence
- sensitivity
- decisiveness
- co-operation
- objectivity.

LOOKING AT THE COMPANY OF THE FUTURE

Core business

The business structure of the future is likely to shift to a **small core base** containing a minimal number of key personnel who are involved in management and development, employed on a full-time basis (see Figure 11). This is likely to lead to outsourcing – contracting work out to a freelance or temporary workforce.

Self-employed and contract workers

Attached to the core business may be a fringe of self-employed people used for specialised projects plus a workforce of personnel on temporary contract for peak periods.

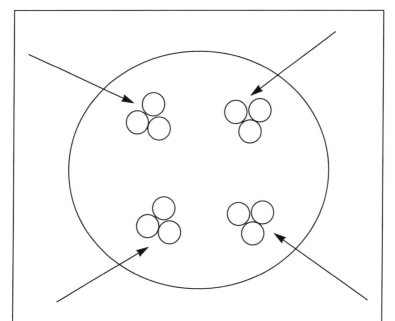

The traditional structure made up of individuals within departments within a company.

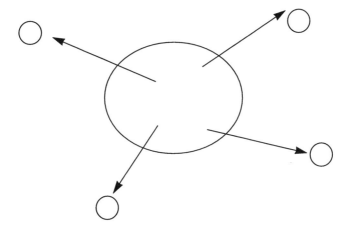

The new structure of outsourcing from a small power-base.

Fig. 11. Traditional and new company structures.

THE LEARNING COMPANY

An increasing philosophy amongst companies is that of the 'Learning Company'.

Traditional company values	*The learning company values*
hierarchy	empowerment
win – lose	co-operation
control-style leadership	win – win
political games	contribution
top-down decisions	responsive to change
distrust	open communication
status-orientated	service
profit-driven	ethics
better than	better at
theory-based business	flexibility

Organisational politics

Organisational politics may be defined as 'the power behind the rules of internal business operations'. Power may be further defined as being:

● personal networks

● behind the scenes decision-making

● formal authority

● bureaucratic empire building

● specific and expert knowledge

● control of technology

● control of the purse strings.

Organisational politics are going to be around for as long as there are organisations. But the future is with the identification, ownership and compassionate use of power so that it becomes empowering to both user and organisation.

Note: It may be part of organisational politics to promote women. But there is the danger that this could be a token promotion in order to be seen as an equal opportunities employer, when in reality the position holds no real responsibilities.

Personal values and corporate values

Most career women tend to sacrifice their personal lives for the top jobs. Professional women are less likely than their male colleagues to marry and have children. Research shows that fatigue, stress and image problems are the main reasons why women in management tend to leave their jobs.

However, there is an increasing contribution of female qualities into the male ethos which has, up to now, largely formed how business operates. The values of women are more closely aligned to those needed by the learning company of the future.

We may believe:

● we lack commitment

● we can't cope with pressure

● we lack organisational skills

● we can't make decisions

● we are not ready for promotion.

We could choose to believe:

● our skills are being enhanced all the time

● our experiences count

● our capabilities are making a positive difference

● our values contribute to the organisational growth

● our achievements are important

● **in ourselves**.

MOVING INTO MANAGEMENT

Management could be viewed as a multifaceted activity which involves specific skills and characteristics. Management is about:

- facilitation

- control

- delegation

- development.

We measure management via:

- processes

- outcomes.

Background management

Managing ourselves

- our thoughts

- our emotions

- our health

- our sexuality

- our appearance.

Interactive management

- our intimate relationships

- our social life.

Managing at home

- our family

- our domestic sphere.

Managing at work

● our money

● our career.

It could take women 500 years before they have equal managerial status with men and a further 475 years before women hold equal political and economic status, according to the International Labour Office of the United Nations.

According to the Institute of Management, the number of women managers has risen. Areas including personnel and marketing tend to have more women at the top than research, manufacturing and production.

An additional problem for women wanting to get into management is the downsizing ethos. Some companies, as they make themselves more cost-effective and productive, are cutting out entire levels of management. Therefore, women who are just one rung below promotion may find that rung entirely missing in their organisation. The next move is either sideways or out of the door.

Workplace management characteristics

valuing others	approachability	fairness
loyalty to staff	challenging yourself	being human
being pro-active	being focused	being creative
admitting your mistakes	taking risks	showing courage
self-expression	being unique	adaptability
co-operation	innovation	resourcefulness
confidence	decisiveness	objectivity

Workplace management skills

selection and recruitment	coaching	counselling
doing appraisals	motivating others	strategic planning
giving feedback	clarifying	managing
giving encouragement	expectations	resources
facilitating change	decision-making	listening
setting objectives	interpersonal	taking action
quality management	skills	managing
skills training	administering	meetings
dealing with conflict	discipline	prioritising
consulting with others	providing energy	time management
working in teams		

Future management skills

According to Skills and Enterprise Network, the skills a manager will need include:

1. A working knowledge of the global market.

2. Coaching.

3. Project management.

4. Counselling.

5. Staff development.

6. Team building.

7. IT management.

8. Languages.

9. Customer service.

10. Managing change.

11. Leading others.

12. Assessing.

Leadership skills

A good manager is a leader of **vision** and **integrity**. She will have the trust of others and will take risks. Women's leadership styles tend to be web-like as opposed to the more male style of a family tree type of leadership. Women are more inclined to balance and share power through empowering others. Men tend to have a hierarchy.

Question time

1. Why do I want promotion?

2. Can I balance my personal life with increased responsibility?

3. Who can I talk to at work?

4. Have I got the basic personal qualities for management?

5. Have I got the staying power?

6. How can I get the professional and personal support I need?

7. What skills do I need to learn?

8. Are there any qualification pathways which could increase my knowledge, skills and confidence?

9. Will my partner and family support me?

10. Do I want to work within someone else's corporate culture?

11. Would I rather work for myself? What ideas have I got?

MOVING INTO DIRECTORSHIPS

The 'glass ceiling' is the term for the elusive step up into senior management or directorship. We can see where we want to go – up! But we can't seem to get there because something is in the way – a lack of skills, knowledge or experience of the old boy's network!

According to a survey by Opportunity 2000, the equal opportunities lobby, the proportion of top British companies with women directors has nearly doubled from eight per cent in 1994 to 15 per cent in 1995.

GETTING TO THE TOP

Women who want influence and power have two choices:

1. Pressuring from within a corporate structure.

2. Self-employment.

Pressuring from within

You could choose to work your way up the corporate ladder and through the management levels. To do this, you will need to be **determined, objective** and **true to yourself**.

The difficulties you face

- the old boy's network

- organisational politics blocking the progress of women

- closed doors

- men being sexist

- women being jealous

- your personal life suffering.

What you could do

- get a woman's development network established within the company

- get a mentor

- get yourself organised

- develop job-specific skills

- gain more knowledge

- be seen as an expert

- unload your frustrations

- join a professional organisation aimed at supporting women in business.

The pay-offs

- the feel-good factor

- status

- kudos

● more money

● control

● power

● contributing to women's role in business.

Running the company

Being self-employed and running your own business is another option. This way, you only have yourself to answer to – you are the top of the tree! You need to have **good business skills, a brilliant idea and staying power**.

The difficulties you face

● selling your services or products

● people saying no

● long hours

● hard work

● fluctuating income

● loneliness.

What you could do

● join support groups for women in business

● diversify your business interests

● outsource.

The pay-offs

● unlimited income

● being in charge

- independence

- unlimited creativity

- choosing your hours of work

- making your mark in commerce or industry.

BALANCING AT THE TOP OF THE TREE

Whether you work for a company or for yourself, the secret to balancing at the top of the tree is using your resources, knowledge, intuition and gut feelings.

Further key points include:

- effective interpersonal skills

- networking

- having a vision and being passionate about that vision

- showing integrity

- trusting others

- taking risks

- understanding that work is just one facet of the whole

- developing long-term goals

- overviewing the entire picture

- unravelling the process of work.

But whatever you are doing, at whatever level, it is crucial to remember that work is only part of the greater whole. You have friends, lovers, partners, family, your home, your social life, your mental and physical health, your pets, leisure time and your dreams. Work is an external representative of who you are – not what you are.

THE CERTIFICATE OF MANAGEMENT RIGHTS

I have the right to:
- speak and be heard
- be respected by my colleagues
- want more
- be in charge
- make my mark in business
- a good income
- the feel-good factor
- kudos
- power
- be seen as an expert
- have support
- challenge myself
- be pro-active
- be creative
- take risks
- express myself
- be unique
- feel confident
- be proud of myself as a woman in business

SIGNED ....

Fig. 12. The certificate of management rights.

The successful, sexy businesswoman
At 35, Jacqueline Gold is the managing director for Ann Summers, the sex-aid and lingerie company. She joined the company in 1980 and introduced the concept of party-plan selling. All of the salesforce and 95 per cent of the head office staff are women.

GOING FOR IT

If you are a woman who wants to go places, you need to be **pro-active**. You need to make things happen. Make opportunities to develop, practise and demonstrate your skills. Create situations for yourself and welcome new experiences. Have higher expectations. Praise yourself. Believe in yourself enough and others will believe in you more. Be prepared to take the rough with the smooth. You can handle your mistakes and you can handle being criticised. If you can't, learn how to!

You can be a woman who is assertive, dynamic and powerful. You are not a female man. You work with men and women who respond to your behaviour, skills, knowledge and experiences in their own way. They have a right to agree or disagree with you. They might not like you. You might not like them. You don't have to like each other. You are there to do a job of work. If you want power, status and a higher income, you must be prepared to expand yourself – but not at the expense of hurting yourself or others.

Checklist

1. Dissect the behaviours and attitudes of women you admire in business. Explore issues about power.

2. To find out more about the company of the future, read Charles Handy.

3. To develop your management potential, either invest in private training or if working, ask to go on training courses.

4. If you wish to run your own company, contact your local Training and Enterprise Council.

CASE STUDIES

Maria sees herself develop

Maria is beginning to realise that her aggressiveness doesn't mean that she is being assertive. She is learning how to define herself while allowing others the same right. Her defensiveness is beginning to break down and a genuinely strong woman is slowly emerging. She acknowledges her ambition and wants to channel this into her own business.

Carol takes a risk

Carol has her eyes firmly on management. Her place of work is part of the Civil Service and has strong organisational policies. However, her particular department encourages women to move up the promotional ladder – at a price. Carol has to often go away on courses which means leaving her husband and young child. She chooses the option of development and hopes her family will support her.

Diane is concerned

Diane is concerned with her age and gaining employment, therefore one strong consideration is self-employment in the field of desktop publishing and design.

DISCUSSION POINTS

1. What makes a career woman?

2. Explore different styles of management and decide which you prefer.

3. If you attended a meeting as a manager with the aim of getting the budget for your department set and you found that your budget levels had been pre-determined without consultation, how would you react?

7
Overcoming Sexual
Harassment and Prejudice

BECOMING AWARE OF YOUR SEXUAL IMAGE

Men tend to operate on a more physical level than women, including a direct response to sex. Women seek to integrate their emotional needs with other aspects of their life including the sexual side of their nature. Traditionally, women have been conditioned to hide their bodies and push back their sexuality. Women tend to hold beliefs about their sexuality which include:

● masturbation is wrong

● women shouldn't enjoy sex

● women shouldn't be seen as the initiator of the sexual act

● women mustn't encourage a man otherwise she may be considered easy

● wearing short or tight skirts means you're a tart

● having large breasts is something to be ashamed of

● women mustn't act provocatively

● if a woman is fat she can't have a sex life.

Defining a male sexual image

1. Ask a man you know to define his sexual image according to himself.

2. Now define his sexual image from your position as a woman.

Defining a female sexual image

1. Define your own sexual image.

2. Now ask another woman to define your sexual image for you.

3. Now ask a man who knows you to define your sexual image for you.

What is feminine?

Femininity could be defined as a set of values which represent the female and a set of behaviours which act out those values. Possible values may include:

- ladies wait to be asked

- we are here to be wives and mothers

- women must support their menfolk.

   Possible behaviours may include:

- wearing flouncy styles

- wearing pastel colours

- when sitting down, crossing the legs at the ankles and slanting the legs to one side

- wearing make-up

- having long hair

- speaking quietly

- keeping your eyes downcast

- waiting for doors to be opened for you.

What is sexy?

According to the media, there are certain styles which are associated with sexual display:

- dangling earrings

- long hair worn loose

- strong perfume

- low necklines.

Looking good

We are told that there are certain styles appropriate for a professional appearance in business:

- wear clothes which don't cling too much

- go for skirts or dresses which don't rise when you sit down

- always wear hosiery even in the summer

- opt for stylish court shoes.

A woman might choose to feel sexy wearing an old sack. An aura of sexuality could come from anyone regardless of what they are wearing. For many women, seeing a man in a well cut suit, cleanly presented and well spoken, might be a turn on. But women are not so inclined to reach for the buttocks as some men might be. If a man is determined to sexually harass a woman at work, he will do so regardless of clothing – although some men might use the excuse of how a woman dresses as inflammatory to his desire.

Exercise

Get some feedback on what image you project through your clothes. A woman who is professionally-minded in her work would be advised to dress:

- in the style in which she feels comfortable

- in a manner which gives her confidence

- according to her working environment

- with reference to how in control and assertive she appears.

HAVING SEXUAL RELATIONSHIPS

Having sexual relations with work colleagues is a tricky area.

Some women seek escape through work. Escape may mean having an affair with a married man or sleeping with the boss. Sex may happen at the Christmas office party in the stationery cupboard. It might happen because of boredom. It might happen as a by-product of an unhappy marriage. A woman might have a sexual relationship at work as a way of proving her power. It may happen as a wild bid for independence. It might even happen for love.

If you choose to have a sexual relationship, take responsibility for your actions and in most cases, be prepared for fallout.

DEALING WITH SEXUAL HARASSMENT

Definitions of sexual harassment

Sexual harassment might apply to lesbians and gay men as well as heterosexual women and men. The first British case to be prosecuted was in 1986, when a female laboratory technician took her employers to court over sexual harassment (and won). That opened the way for other women to take cases to court under the Sex Discrimination Act.

Sexual harassment does not have to involve sexual desire. But if the comments or behaviour reflect your gender and makes you feel uncomfortable then it becomes sexual harassment.

How does it happen?

Broadly speaking, sexual harassment is more common for women than for men and tends to occur where there is a major difference in status between individuals within the workplace. It can take the following forms:

- the boss who promises promotion in return for sexual favours or demotion if not complied with

- unnecessary body contact

- the office junior given a difficult time by the adult males in the office

- offensive pin-ups

- degrading remarks

- crude comments about personal appearance

- the woman manager given a difficult time by a male subordinate

- sexual jokes

- the male group who ridicule a woman entering a male-dominated workplace.

Why does it happen?

There are a number of reasons why sexual harassment occurs. Primarily it springs from negative and ignorant beliefs which some men are conditioned to, such as:

- the perception that women are sex objects derived from media presentation and role model behaviour

- the abuse of power over an apparently weaker sex

- a bully can enjoy tormenting someone weaker than themselves

- it is OK to humiliate women

- it is justifiable to control women

- males should stick together and prove their manhood by under-mining women

- men are superior and women are inferior

- women should be submissive not equal

- men make the law

- the workplace is a male domain.

The emotional backlash

When sexual harassment occurs in the workplace, there could be any number of backlashes including being fired or not receiving promotion. An unseen backlash is the emotional distress which is caused.

Humiliation

If the sexual harassment occurs in front of other staff, the humiliation is increased – it becomes public. The abuse is patronising and abusive. Your reaction could be one of lashing out to embarrass him publicly or you might accept it and seethe inwardly.

Vulnerability

Sexual harassment is an invasion of your body space. Someone has handled you regardless of your thoughts or feelings. In fact, there is likely to be the assumption that you haven't any – that you want it, like it or have asked for it.

Fear

The ultimate fear we have is one of violation. We fear being overwhelmed, hurt and raped.

Anger

The anger comes from the invasion, the arrogance, the thoughtlessness, the assumption, the abuse of power and authority.

Depression

Depression tends to occur when anger turns inward against the self. Did I lead him on? Was I asking for it? What can I do? I may lose my job if I ask for help.

Anxiety

As all these emotions swim round in our head, we still try to do our job. We go home – we may talk to a friend. We may talk to no one. We start believing we deserve it. We want to keep our job. It happens again. We want to hit out. We need our job.

Powerlessness

Sexual harassment can make us feel tied up in knots. Someone is saying or doing something to us without our permission. We feel humiliated and belittled. We might try to answer back – maybe we get laughed at.

Undermining confidence

If we are being sexually harassed, it means our position as a woman is being ridiculed. We are not being taken seriously. Our work position is not being taken seriously. It means we are not being acknowledged as a human being with rights or abilities.

> **No one can take away from you**
> **that which you give away yourself**

If you are being sexually harassed, there are a number of options open to you. Ultimately, you have the freedom to vote with your feet and leave the job. You can always get another job, but it will be more difficult to build up shattered confidence if you stay and accept the abuse.

What the law says

'This code of practice will be a source of great clarity, comfort and confidence-building to victims now experiencing harassment. It marks a real step forward for working women in the 1990s in Europe. The labour market of the 1990s, the changes that are going on within it and the present skills shortage will mean that more women will be present at the workplace than ever before in the years to come. While that may mean more incidents of harassment it should also mean that women will have more influence to demand a strengthening of the national laws to combat harassment.' Christine Crawley MEP, addressing the European Parliament in October 1991.

It can be illegal for an employer not to take action upon complaint.

The Department of Employment publish a booklet called *Sexual Harassment in the Workplace: A guide for employers*.

What you can do about it

The law may be on your side, but you can also do a number of things yourself. Being pro-active will give you a sense of control and power. You could try:

● keeping a record of the circumstances of the sexual harassment incidents (date, location, nature of incident, any witnesses)

● talking to women colleagues – you may find several other people have experienced sexual harassment from the same person

● getting outside support from friends, family, doctor, partner or a women's group

● making sure there are other people around if you have to work late with the harasser

- reporting the harasser to your manager, superior or personnel

- taking an assertiveness or self-defence course which will help you speak your mind with authority

- confronting the harasser, with your colleagues or with a senior member of staff or union representative – tell the harasser that you dislike his behaviour and you want him to stop

- reporting any indecent assault to the police

- reporting the harasser to the Equal Opportunities Commission

- writing a letter of complaint to the harasser

- taking down offensive pin-ups or putting up pictures of naked men.

Other routes to stopping harassment, if you feel confident enough:

- embarrass him – if he pats your bum, pat his crotch

- treat him like a parent treats a naughty child – tell him off loudly and publicly

- make a joke of it.

Don't bottle it up – tell someone

CHALLENGING PREJUDICE

Prejudice in the workplace could come from men or other women.

Traditionally, men regard the workplace as a male-dominated area and as more women enter the world of commerce and industry, resentment and confusion is going to increase.

Women are still formulating their work identity. Someone once said to me 'women don't have friends, they have competitors'. For a large part, this is true in the workplace, especially in positions of authority and power.

It takes tact, diplomacy, staying power and skill to balance the line of prejudice while still being true to yourself.

Transforming negative attitudes

You have no control over another person's attitude or beliefs. But you have control over your own. By your own thoughts, feelings and behaviours, you give an impression to your colleagues, superiors and subordinates of who you are.

If you work with bigoted people who try to belittle you, put you down, harass you or take away your power, it is up to you to keep faith with yourself. It goes something like this:

Thought	– John is trying to undermine my authority by telling me I can't do my work when I know I can
Feeling	– frustration, anger
Choice	– blow my top or take control
Decision	– to go to my boss and get his or her support
	– to tell John assertively that my work is my responsibility
Experience	– self-respect
	– my work under my control
	– a work colleague knows he or she can't ride rough-shod over me
	– confidence in the support of my boss.

When people see you behaving assertively and with confidence they have two choices. They can either respect you, however grudgingly, or they can carry on in their bigoted way. Just because you play by a set of fair rules, doesn't necessarily mean other people will. Hopefully they will but if they don't, you then have two choices. To accept the way they are and to carry on being assertive, knowing that life won't always be easy with them, or to get away from them. You've got the power. You decide.

Working with patriarchs

A patriarchal society is a male-dominated culture. Attitudes may include:

● male values rule, *eg* wealth, competition and aggression

● men are leaders while women follow

● it's OK for a woman to gain power by default, *eg* Indira Ghandi

● the male has a greater value than the female.

Women's support

To a greater extent, women have supported a patriarchal society. Women have believed that they need to be protected, that they have a limited value and that it is wrong to have a position of power by merit alone. Women tend to collude by putting others first, maintaining harmony, by doing much of society's unpaid work and by being the backbone of family and working man.

Some tips on how to cope with patriarchs:

- limit contact time

- get on with the job

- when you have contact time, deal in facts, calmly and assertively

- stay in control

- you don't have to prove anything

- get support from other superiors

- he's not your father – don't feel like a child

- remember that you are a skilled woman in your own right.

Working with other women

Women can be bitchy and underhand. With a man in business, you usually know where you stand, although there are exceptions to the rule. Most women in positions of authority are up front but again there are exceptions. There is often a sense of betrayal when a woman does something behind your back – somehow it isn't something you expect from your own gender. But it does happen. Again, you need to have your rules to play by. You need to formulate your own ethos and relevant behaviour. Suggestions might include:

- be direct

- be firm

- have confident body language

- have a support network

- don't be frightened to ask for help

- know your facts

- be prepared to confront.

Prejudice and sexual harassment exist. For both genders, from both genders. It is the individual's responsibility to take action decisively. Ask for support if necessary. Know what you are talking about. Take control quickly.

You are a woman at work. Everyone has rights. You have a mind to think and a mouth to speak. Don't put up with behaviour from others which you find offensive or distressing. Life's too short to spend it worrying about how another person is hurting you.

Checklist

1. Get the view from men and women you know, about how your sexual image comes across.

2. Get the view from men and women you know, about the image your clothes give.

3. Use your power to confront men who sexually harass you.

4. You only have control over yourself. Don't fall into playing power games with others. Don't start acting out your childish fantasies in the workplace. Behave like an adult and get on with the job.

CASE STUDIES

Maria has a 'little girl' approach

Maria has a mass of dark hair, large brown eyes and likes to wear short lycra skirts. She is very much caught up in the mating game in her private life and tends to see the working environment as another catchment area. She had one incident of sexual harassment from a substantially older boss who kept hinting at after-work dates. Maria's way of handling it was to keep him dangling with sheer cheek.

Carol is in charge

Carol is a large lady and uses her size with pride. There is a fairly casual dress code where she works and because the client base is largely male, Carol has had plenty of opportunities to refine her technique for dealing with sexist remarks. If the remarks are directly abusive, she reacts in a more parental way in dealing with it. If the comments are mildly flirtatious, she responds in kind. She works in an environment that employs a large amount of gay personnel.

Diane is self-conscious

The printing company Diane has worked in is male-dominated, although her section employed two other women. There was a protective sense about the group of women in the midst of intense male prejudice. Now in her 40s and considering self-employment, Diane is very self-conscious about her appearance and whether she can appear professional enough.

DISCUSSION POINTS

1. How would you respond to a woman colleague who dressed sexily?

2. What has the patriarchal society given the world?

3. What do the men around you think women find sexually offensive?

8
Breakthrough not Breakdown

DEFINING STRESS

Stress is not caused by an event, but by our response to the event.

We need a certain amount of stress to get the adrenaline pumping. **Positive stress** situations may include seeing an old friend after several years' separation, going to a party or receiving an award. **Negative stress** is when our response to a situation is overwhelming us and getting out of hand. If we turn to artificial stimulants or props to help us through situations, we are allowing our thoughts and feelings to control our behaviours.

When we are young, we are taught not to be afraid. We get the message that fear is not acceptable or desirable if we want to get on in life. Consequently, we grow up developing unconscious coping strategies for when we become fearful or anxious. We may learn to:

● numb our feelings

● eat our way to comfort

● drink ourselves into false confidence

● take drugs to induce a rosy glow

● bury ourselves in activity.

Self-acceptance

We need to understand and accept that it is OK not to feel OK. We can feel anxious or frightened and still push through it to do what is causing us distress. We may need support, we may need to cry, we may need to be held in order to see it through – but we can still feel the fear and do it anyway.

There are times when the levels of fear, anxiety and tension become unbearable and cause us to feel negative or react irrationally. If intense negativity is allowed to take a hold, it can affect the immune system which keeps us free from infection and illness. When the immune system becomes weakened, we become ill. Stress affects the body and if our mental state persists in its anxious mode for too long, we may get a minor or even a major illness.

Cycle of stress

We need to look at three basic stages in order to identify the levels of stress:

1. Physical symptoms.

2. Psychological symptoms.

3. Stress-prone beliefs.

We can experience stress in relation to any area of our life including work. As a working woman, you are particularly vulnerable because of the many roles you balance. Therefore the next stage involves identifying job stress triggers and your thought process behind them, your coping strategy and outcome.

There is a negative or a positive way to handle stress and our choice of how we deal with it is based on:

- our conditioned response (learnt from early role models, *eg* how mum handled anxiety)

- our levels of control (emotional and mental)

- our behaviourial skills (*eg* making time, being assertive).

Identifying job stress

Whatever your job, there are particular areas that give you more pleasure, others which you do purely by rote and others which cause varying degrees of stress. Figure 13 gives you an opportunity to identify some areas of pressure in your own job.

IDENTIFYING PHYSICAL STRESS

When we are anxious, our body produces various symptoms, which in themselves are fairly harmless.

Issue	Yes	No
I feel I have a lack of control over responsibilities and duties.		
I am often caught in conflicting situations with co-workers.		
I have a low salary with limited raises.		
I have too much to do.		
I am working in a hazardous or unpleasant environment.		
I cannot see how to advance professionally.		
I have to do or say things which are against my personal belief system.		
I have to work to deadlines most of the time.		
I am lacking in knowledge for the job I have to do.		
I am not feeling challenged enough.		
I have unsupportive superiors.		
I do not feel valued or appreciated.		
I have a sense of being overwhelmed by the larger organisation.		
I have a lot of travelling to do in connection with my work.		
I am finding it hard to be a working mother.		
I am being sexually harassed at work.		
There are threats of redundancy in the air.		
I have to give a lot of presentations.		
I take my work home with me.		
I haven't had a holiday for over 12 months.		
I am being discriminated against.		
I feel trapped.		

Fig. 13. Identifying job pressures.

When we undergo intense stress, we may experience symptoms which are more distressing or long-term.

If you are concerned about any physical symptom, please go to your doctor or health practitioner.

Assessing your physical symptoms

Tick any symptoms which you have been experiencing noticeably for longer than two months.

tired	....	low sex drive	....
physically depleted	....	overeating	....
drinking more	....	smoking more	....
taking abusive drugs	....	increased illness	....
high blood pressure	....	tension headaches	....
indigestion	....	stomach ulcers	....
rashes	....	palpitations	....
erratic bowel movements	....	insomnia	....
muscular aches and pains	....	teeth grinding	....
allergies	....	shallow breathing	....
sudden weight loss or gain	....	dry mouth and throat	....
nightmares	....	altered menstrual cycle	....
excessive sweating	....	dizziness	....
trembling	....	twitching	....
stuttering	....	high pitched laughter	....
excessive throat swallowing	....	hypermobility	....
weakness	....	heaviness of limbs	....
chest pains	....	fidgeting	....
butterflies	....	faster breathing	....

The more ticks, the higher your current stress levels.

Relaxation

The art of physical relaxation is getting out of the head and into the body. When we place our awareness in our body, our mind separates from mental chit-chat, focuses and slows down.

Progressive relaxation

This form of relaxation focuses on each part of the body in turn and works on the principle of tensing each muscle group and then releasing the tension to demonstrate muscular relaxation.

Autogenic training
During this exercise, you imagine that each muscle group is becoming warm and heavy thereby leading to physical relaxation.

Biofeedback
This is a small hand-held machine which responds with varying degrees of noise to your physical symptoms of stress. When you are tense, the machine makes a high-pitched sound and when you are relaxed, the sound of the machine is low. The idea is to do relaxation exercises and to let the machine monitor your progress.

Deep breathing
Tense breathing occurs from the upper chest and is rapid and shallow. Relaxed breathing involves inhaling and exhaling slowly from the stomach and diaphragm. The outbreath is always longer than the inbreath.

Physically releasing stress
A physical release channels the psychological frustration into action. It can act as a catalyst for a more creative space. You could:

● do aerobic sport such as swimming or cycling

● punch a cushion

● have a massage (give a massage)

● take part in recreational sport

● do yoga

● go for a brisk walk

● make love

● cry.

Nutrition
Part of a stressful lifestyle is not making enough time to eat and not

eating the right food or taking enough of the right nutrition. Some tips include:

- eat plenty of fibre

- eat plenty of fresh vegetables and fruit

- have a low-fat diet

- increase your vitamin B and C intake

- take Siberian ginseng for mental upkeep

- take Korean ginseng for physical upkeep

- avocado, lentils and spinach are good foods for fatigue

- if you suffer from low blood sugar eat small and regular meals of protein

- eat bread, potato or pasta for long-lasting energy.

IDENTIFYING PSYCHOLOGICAL STRESS

Our psychological make-up consists of our mental and emotional well-being and is the foundation for our physical stress symptoms.

Assessing your psychological symptoms

Tick any symptoms which you have been experiencing noticeably for longer than two months.

little enthusiasm	....	frustration	....
moodiness	....	irritability	....
need to withdraw	....	feeling negative	....
depression	....	dissatisfaction	....
boredom	....	forgetfulness	....
easily discouraged	....	irrational crying	....
self-doubt	....	apathy	....
confusion	....	intolerance	....
resentment	....	distrust	....
cynicism	....	feeling lonely	....

indecisiveness	....	lack of concentration	....
procrastination	....	fearfulness	....
emotional outbursts	....	unable to switch off	....

The more ticks, the higher your current stress levels.

COUNTERING A STRESS-PRONE BELIEF SYSTEM

This represents the underlying beliefs we have about ourselves and our place in the world.

Assessing your stress-prone beliefs

Tick those beliefs which you feel apply to you.

I forget appointments.	....
I can never seem to catch up with myself.	....
Everything I do must be perfect.	....
I can't trust others to do a job as well as I can do it.	....
I always seem negative.	....
I don't seem to have anyone who cares about me.	....
I always do what other people want.	....
I mustn't fail.	....
I can't laugh at myself.	....
I always take on more work than I can handle.	....
I can never seem to sit still.	....
I find it hard to just daydream.	....
I always have to have an end goal in what I do.	....
I avoid intimacy.	....
I hate being alone.	....
I experience phobias.	....
I think of myself as less worthwhile than others.	....
I feel I have little control over my life.	....
I feel overwhelmed when things go wrong.	....
I feel anxious when the unforseen occurs.	....
I blame others when things go wrong.	....
I avoid taking responsibility for myself or my life.	....

Positive mental attitudes

Our mental attitude underlies our feelings. However, we tend to be more aware of our feelings than our thoughts. We can be aware of feeling shy, depressed or anxious, but we are not necessarily aware of the thought that precedes the feeling.

Our unconscious thoughts are part of our belief system which is formed at a young age by influences such as parents, other members of the family, teachers, the media and friends.

There is a fear in our society of mental illness and breakdown. These states are seen as shameful and something to be hidden away. In reality, a change in the state of consciousness which a breakdown can bring about can be both enlightening and releasing. Who is to determine the difference between madness and sanity? There are chemical definitions, but at the end of the day, providing that the individual is not a danger to him/herself or others, who is of the right mind to define the difference?

A positive mental attitude is one which makes you feel:

- confident

- motivated

- excited

- happy

- alive.

Developing a positive mental attitude takes conscious thinking. Instead of having the vague thought 'I am bored with this job' and feeling apathetic, you could deliberately think 'I am now ready for a new challenge. I am getting ready to move on and have feelings of anticipation and hope'.

Coping with change

When we feel stressed out, it could be because we are stuck. Stuck in saying yes, stuck in a dead-end job, stuck with dissatisfaction. But in order to feel better, we have to risk change. We have to let go of the old and take on the new. Often we prefer the devil we know – even though we moan and are unhappy. But if we stay stuck, we will never know what could be round the corner and although we fear it being worse – it could be better. Is your glass half full or half empty?

Expressing your feelings

We may be able to control our thoughts, but controlling our feelings is another matter entirely. They seem to have a life of their own. It is socially acceptable for women to be emotional and for men to have a stronger thought process. But life is about balance for both sexes. It is OK for men to be sensitive and to express their emotions and it is OK for women to develop their thinking skills. The business of the future depends upon it.

Stress is an inappropriate implosion of driven emotions based on fear. Stress is considerably diluted by the appropriate expression of emotional tension. Suggestions could include:

●   not suppressing your feelings

●   acknowledging them to yourself and others

●   learning to be adaptable

●   talking it out

●   writing it out.

Saying no

An overload of stress could occur because you keep saying yes to the demands of other people, or to what you think other people are demanding of you. Assertiveness training will help you to:

●   become aware of your boundaries

●   set new boundaries

●   define yourself

●   take responsibility for yourself

●   deal with criticism

●   confront difficult situations

●   solve problems

●   develop new behaviourial skills for confidence.

As part of saying no, you may need to consider taking a career break or changing job.

Job stress trigger:	Your yearly appraisal out of which comes your pay rise
Physical symptoms:	Frontal headaches, tired eyes, tense jaw, clenched muscles
Psychological symptoms:	Perfectionism, fretfulness
Stress-prone beliefs:	'They'll sack me if I'm not good enough'

	Negative	Positive
Thought process:	– I hate this. I'll get a rotten pay rise. She will just criticise me.	– I have some constructive things I would like to say to my boss. I look forward to hearing the areas I could improve upon. This is an opportunity to show my boss my enthusiasm.
Coping strategy:	– defensiveness – lack of co-operation	– knowing which areas you need to improve upon – negotiation skills
Outcome:	– resentment against your boss – unspoken hurts – dissatisfaction with your job	– pay rise – knowledge of areas to improve – self-respect – open communication with your boss

Fig. 14. A job stress scenario.

Meditation

The art of meditation is control of the mind. Your local adult education college will have several meditation classes on offer. A typical course involves physical relaxation, deep breathing and instruction on different techniques to focus and relax the mind. As you become proficient at meditation, you can use the skills anywhere – the bus stop, during your lunchbreak or sitting on the train.

NETWORKING FOR SUPPORT

Networking is the art of **making contact** with others. Women are good at networking – they tend to build the social contacts. However, networking is a major part of a successful working life as well. We network for support, information, job opportunities and advice. We might network using membership contacts, contacts from past employment, our counterparts in other companies, our superiors, our peers and personal contacts. When networking:

● ask for direct help

● tell others that you value their support

● support others in return – you know what it feels like to need help.

Figure 15 will give you a start in building a list of contacts.

MANAGING YOUR TIME

Time management is the art of **organising** and **prioritising** your tasks.

As a working woman, your time is precious. Work is one part of your life. You have others to balance as well including caring for yourself.

I am not suggesting that you should be all things to all people or that you should do everything. This is where we need to learn to ask for support or delegate. A working woman has to manage her time effectively for her own sake – not anyone else's.

Assessing your time

● Make a timetable for three days of what you do and the times that you do it.

My professional network contact list

Telephone number

Line manager:

Personnel officer:

Member of women's group/organisation:

Mentor:

Career counsellor:

Others:

My personal network contact list

Telephone number

Friend:

Partner:

Family:

Counsellor:

Others:

Fig. 15. Network contact lists.

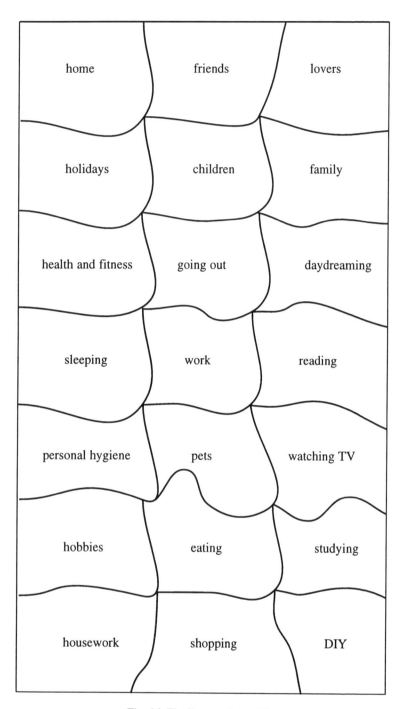

Fig. 16. The jigsaw of your life.

(The spot marked with an x is your reminder.)

	At work	At home
Make a 'to do' list every day	x	x
Prioritise my daily work	x	x
Do one task at a time	x	x
Prepare for meetings	x	
make my phone calls brief	x	x
Delegate where possible	x	x
Don't over-commit myself	x	x
Know my limitations	x	x
Make sure each task is necessary	x	x
Look for faster methods and better procedures	x	
Don't procrastinate – do it now	x	x
Deal with it or dump it – don't hoard it	x	x
Complete tasks before putting them down	x	x
Set aside time each day for call-backs	x	
Avoid people who take advantage	x	x
Decide if that meeting is an opportunity or a time waster	x	
Discipline myself	x	x
Monitor my progress daily	x	
Set myself objectives	x	x
Learn to say no	x	x
Stop being a perfectionist	x	x

Fig. 17. Time management reminder list.

- How much of your time do you spend doing things for other people who could do it for themselves?

- How much of what you do is actually unnecessary?

- Is there anything you can let go of?

It is possible to enjoy stress and to get a buzz from the adrenaline pumping. But it is your responsibility to assess when it is becoming detrimental to your mental, emotional and physical health. Identify your source of stress, develop constructive strategies and practise them.

Nurturing yourself means treating yourself like your own best friend. It means making time to be with yourself and by yourself. It means giving yourself mental brownie points for what you have done and loving yourself in spite of what you haven't done.

Breaking through, not breaking down, means developing and using your **self-awareness** to reach greater heights of personal knowledge and fulfilment. Sometimes the old methods of coping have to fail before we understand and accept the right way of being.

Checklist

1. To help identify job stress, keep a daily work journal.

2. Become aware of what your body is saying to you. Listen and respond. Find 15 minutes a day to do some physical relaxation. Don't eat on the run. Eat healthy food – but don't die of boredom.

3. Remember, your mind needs a change of scenery every day. Try to maintain a positive mental attitude. Keep connected to your feelings – it means you're alive.

4. Learn meditation.

5. Build a network. Ask for help – and offer it.

6. Build time into every day for a little playtime.

CASE STUDIES

Maria skims the surface

Maria is a hyperactive person who thrives on action. Often she makes the wrong decision based on the fear of being inactive. She believes she is good at coping with change, but in reality, she is scared of commitment. Her diet is healthy and she enjoys good health but she hates to be still and doesn't allow herself enough space to think and plan.

Carol deceives herself

Carol's job is very stressful as she deals all day with people who are unemployed. She has to be constantly ready for anything or to take charge if an incident occurs. As a working mother, she can't switch off easily when she gets home, although her partner does help out. She is learning to be more direct and honest with her communication which is cutting out misunderstandings. However, when it comes to issues which affect her personally, she is very good at deceiving herself. Carol often gets colds and sniffles and recently her menstrual cycle has changed regularity.

Diane is a worry-bucket

Diane lacks confidence in defining herself out of a safe structure. When she knows something well, she is confident but doesn't venture beyond the known. She tends to comfort eat when anxious and suffers from a sensitive 'worry-bucket' stomach.

DISCUSSION POINTS

1.   What are the positive aspects of stress?

2.   What aspects of work in general have caused or are currently causing you undue stress?

3.   Define a healthy mental attitude.

9
Organising Your Work Strategy

BALANCING HOME AND WORK

Women have a number of roles to balance, especially if they work. No one person can do everything and the art of delegation is as much a fact of life at home as it is at work.

Delegating responsibilities

It is no longer just the woman who keeps the home fires burning. It is a co-operative effort. When your partner takes on his responsibilities around the home, you don't have to thank him for helping you. You are working together as equals for domestic comfort. As women take on more external roles, the internal running of a home has to be shared – that way we all learn!

Housework
A quick tidy-up every day. A major clean once a week can be done in under two hours. Get the kids to keep their rooms clean by bribing them with a reward. You won't lose social status by having a little dust around the place!

DIY
Make a list. Your partner may enjoy doing particular tasks. Why don't you expand your skills? Bring in an expert and pay them.

Elderly and adult dependents
Options may include social services, community care, delegation of care with partner and family or consider working from home.

Shopping
Your partner could develop skills through learning to budget and shop. Plan in advance.

Cooking
Get a freezer and buy in bulk. Don't waste time buying non-essentials every day.

Looking after pets
A good way for children to learn responsibility. Get a pet that is fairly self-sufficient. Alternatively don't have any.

Laundry
Use the washing machine overnight. Leave the washing down the launderette for a service wash.

Car maintenance
Take a course yourself. Get a couple of good, regular mechanics you can call on. Looking after your car regularly will cut down on costs.

Crucial incidentals
These ones are down to you:

● time to relax

● time with children

● time with your partner

● time for hobbies

● time with friends

● time for exercise.

Childcare
Mothers help
Will do housework as well as childcare but may be young and unqualified. Cost around £80-£100 per week.

Partner
A familiar face who knows the routine intimately, will also provide a meaningful insight into role reversal. Cost is likely to include listening to his day.

Relatives
Provides a familiar and loving face but you may feel they could interfere too easily.

Au pairs
Will do housework as well as childcare plus introducing child to other cultures but you will have a lack of privacy within your home and they probably won't stay long. Costs around £40-£60 per week.

Nannies
Should be qualified and will work in your own home; you gain flexible hours and individual care but you are likely to lose privacy within your home. Costs between £100 and £200 per week depending on whether they live in.

Childminders
Someone who has been vetted and is registered with social services but you will have to take your child to and from the childminder's premises. Costs may vary between £50 and £90 per week.

Friends
Familiar face you can trust but you may feel in their debt. Cost could be a box of chocolates or a bottle of wine.

Nursery school and playgroups
Pre-primary school environment. Costs vary.

Public nurseries
These will be local and open throughout the year. May suit if you don't work full-time. Low costs as they are normally subsidised.

Private/workplace nurseries
Run by qualified staff on well equipped premises but there are few nursery spaces available and small babies may not get the best of attention. Costs vary between £80 and £140 per week.

Out-of-school clubs
Occurs on school premises after school until around 6pm, all day during holidays with good supervision and fun content but there are waiting lists. Costs around £20 per week.

Employer/nursery partnership
Employers share the capital and revenue costs.

Placing a value on role reversal

Gender reversal is alive and well and living in many homes. Due to the changing face of work and new trends emerging, it is becoming easier for women to get work than men in some respects. Whatever the work, whether it is paid or unpaid, there is a value in the doing of it and the achievement. When we get paid for a job, we are getting acknowledged through money; when we do an unpaid job, it is nice to get paid in appreciation.

GETTING YOUR MONEY'S WORTH

Earning more than your partner

Traditionally men have been conditioned to earn the money while women maintain hearth and home. Nowadays, the woman is out there, developing skills while the man wonders where his job has gone. According to research by Essex University, in one in five couples today the woman earns more than the man.

Because of the increase in opportunities in the service sector and flexible working conditions, the familiar male working structure is disappearing. Non-traditional roles are becoming a very real part of our lives. There is a blurring, a cross-over of expectations and roles from both genders.

Getting what you're worth

Do you know what you are financially worth? Men still tend to be paid higher for the same job as a woman.

> **Women make up 43 per cent of the labour force**
> **but earn wages on average one third less than men**

Traditionally men are seen as hunters, the breadwinners, the leaders, the more outwardly powerful and aggressive of the sexes. Because of the stereotype vision of women as nurturing and passive, there is the mistaken belief that a caring attitude rules out wanting a good salary for the job, which leads to lower wages for women. This is unbalanced and negative. You have the right to a good salary, equal to a man doing the same job, and to have a regular rise.

MARKETING YOURSELF

If you are seeking a new job, looking for promotion or returning to the workplace, you are in the position of selling your:

- **Skills** – practical things you can do, *eg* word processing

- **Knowledge** – the information you have in your mind, *eg* the process necessary to design a newsletter

- **Strengths** – personal qualities, *eg* tact, humour

- **Experience** – your working (and life) experience.

Identifying your market

When you have assessed your skills and strengths, you are then ready to begin identifying your market.

Ask yourself:

- What type of job do I want?

- What kind of working environment?

- Do I want promotion?

- What kind of values are important to me at work?

- What do I want from an employer?

- Would I be selling to clients and customers as a self-employed woman?

- Why do I want to work for a particular type of company?

- Are the companies I want to work for going places?

Creating opportunities

The four most common ways of getting a job are:

- agencies

- speculative letters

- word of mouth

- advertised vacancies.

Reading between the lines

When you are looking for a new job, it is important to understand the **job specification**. There are two ways to read job specs: the 'stated' and the 'hidden'. Stated means literally the words on the page. Hidden means reading between the lines for the skills, strengths and knowledge not immediately apparent.

Stated   Full-time receptionist required for a busy doctor's practice. Good administration skills necessary and word processing experience desirable.

Hidden   Someone who is sympathetic and likes working with the public. Someone who is tactful, good under pressure and who can reassure patients. Someone who looks smart and approachable. Someone who is organised and computer literate.

If you can read the hidden requirements for a job description, this could put you ahead of your competitors who just scan the obvious.

Writing your CV

A **curriculum vitae** is your work history. You need your CV to sell yourself to a potential employer.

Some tips for a better CV

- make sure it's no longer than two A4 pages

- have it typewritten or word processed

- be brief

- make sure it contains only relevant information

- use action words to describe your skills, *eg* diagnosed, administered, organised

- when writing about your employment history, start with what you are doing now and work back

- avoid words such as 'unemployed'

- fill in gaps in employment by describing any courses or voluntary work you have done

- use short sentences

- detail the year of employment, not the month

- always start your CV with personal details, *eg* name, address and telephone number

- there is no need to include age, marital status or nationality

- include a personal profile: three or four sentences which describe relevant key skills, strengths and experiences

- employers like to hear from people who have achieved things, *eg* cut costs, increased turnover, avoided potential problems

- bear in mind the impression your hobbies will make on the potential employer

- additional information may include driving experience, languages, community activities, ability to work unsociable hours, club membership

- when detailing past employment write down the skills you used within each job.

Writing letters

When job hunting, there are two types of **letters** you need to have skill in writing.

A covering letter

This is used in response to an advertised vacancy. You may be asked to send your CV in or to apply in writing. The covering letter is the vital first impression document. If you can hook the reader through this one page and they turn over to see your CV, the next step could be an inter-view. If you fluff the letter, the motivation to turn over the page could be lost.

A speculative letter
This is 'cold-calling in writing'. It is a letter sent to a named individual in a company. You are not asking for a job, although that is the bottom line. You are asking for information regarding opportunities. You need to research the company and identify where you could fit in. You finish the letter on a positive note by asking for a meeting – not an interview.

When you send a speculative letter, you are unlikely to be facing the kind of competition that you would be by sending in your CV and a covering letter to an advertised vacancy. You may be one of only two or three when sending in a spec letter. Further advantages of spec letters may be:

● your letter may arrive at the right time as a vacancy arises (more vacancies are filled through spec approaches and word of mouth than through advertisements)

● your letter and CV go on file for reference when a vacancy does occur

● your skills, strengths and experience plus your spec letter are so impressive, you actually create a need in the company to take you on board.

Figures 18 and 19 show examples of covering and speculative letters.

Interview techniques
Before the interview

Preparation is the key word prior to an interview. You could:

● research the company using the media, contact or a site visit

● get a full job description (read for the hidden requirements)

● prepare some intelligent questions to ask

● organise what you are going to wear

```
Name                                    Your address
Company name
Address
                                        Your Tel no.
                                        Date


Dear xxxx

Re: Position of Receptionist/Administrator

(First paragraph – what you are writing about)
I would like to apply for the above position as advertised in the
Evening Post on 17 July 199X.

(Second paragraph – your skills, strengths and experience as
relevant to the position you are applying for)
I am currently working for Adams and Sons Solicitors as a full-time
receptionist and have been in this position for two years. Your
vacancy interests me as I have recently finished my NVQ Business
Administration Level 2 and would like to use my developing skills
within a challenging environment.

(Paragraph three – signing off)
I have enclosed my CV for your interest and am available for
interview at any time.

(Note – if you are addressing the letter to a Dear Sir/Madam, sign off
'faithfully'; if you do know the name of the person, sign off
'sincerely')

Yours sincerely/faithfully


(your signature)

MARY SMITH

(if you enclose anything other than a letter in an envelope, put ENC.
at the end of the page).

ENC.
```

Fig. 18. A sample covering letter.

Name   Your address
Company name
Address
                                        Your Tel no.
                                        Date

Dear xxxx

(*First paragraph – who you are and why you are writing*)
I am currently working as a full-time receptionist for Adams and Sons Solicitors and would like the opportunity to expand my horizons within a challenging environment.

(*Second paragraph – your sales pitch - relevant skills, strengths and experience*)
My responsibilities have increased substantially over the past two years to include business administration (NVQ Level 2) and operating computer systems, specifically Word for Windows and Excel.

(*Paragraph three – signing off*)
I would welcome the opportunity of meeting you and enclose my CV for your interest. Please do not hesitate to contact me if I may be of help.

(*Note* – if you are addressing the letter to a Dear Sir/Madam, sign off 'faithfully'; if you do know the name of the person, sign off 'sincerely')

Yours sincerely/faithfully

(your signature)

MARY SMITH

(if you enclose anything other than a letter in an envelope, put ENC. at the end of the page).

ENC.

Fig. 19. A sample speculative letter.

- improve your communication skills

- prepare for the interviewer's questions

- think positive.

During the interview
Some general pointers to help you

- maintain direct eye contact with the interviewer and use his/her name

- smile occasionally

- make your answer relevant to the questions and don't side-track

- avoid waffling

- don't criticise previous employers

- avoid the words 'only' and 'just'

- you are in control

- talk about what you have done

- talk about what you can do

- provides examples of your skills and strengths from past jobs

- don't speak for longer than 30 seconds without a pause

- watch the interviewer's reactions

- look interested

- concentrate

- turn things round to your advantage – you can retrieve a potential disaster if you think

- volunteer appropriate information.

Questions you might be asked

- Why did you leave your last job?

- Why do you want to work for this company?

- What were you doing when you were unemployed?

- Are there any people you find difficulty working with?

- What do you think this job is about?

- How could you contribute to our success?

- What do you consider to be your main strengths?

- What are your weaknesses?

Questions you could ask

- What kind of computer systems do you use?

- What kind of training might I expect?

- What are the routes for staff development?

After the interview

Remember you are still under scrutiny until you are out of the building, up the road and round the corner. Some self-assessment after an interview is always useful. Remember, too, that one interview is now under the belt and it is time to move on. Keep on applying for other jobs. If you are working, do that job to the best of your ability while maintaining your jobsearch. Keep going. Don't stop just because you had an interview. Whether it went well or not, hopefully you will learn from it and apply your discoveries the next time. Keep going.

Checklist

1. Explore the childcare options for working parents in your area. Consider starting up a working parent childcare group.

2. Talk to your partner about how each of your working roles have changed.

3. Get a good "How To" book and write your own CV. Alternatively there are several agencies who advertise CV design in the local press or *Yellow Pages*.

4. Practise your interview techniques with a friend. Video yourself.

CASE STUDIES

Maria settles to study

Maria has no responsibilities at present, although she is now seriously considering sharing a flat with a friend. She is beginning to recognise that she is going to have to find some commitment to a permanent job or career in order to move on in life and have financial independence. She has started a media studies course at college and is working part-time as an administrator/secretary with an advertising company. She is also doing a distance learning course in business skills to prepare for self-employment.

Carol plays the waiting game

Carol's partner takes an active part in running the home and sharing the childcare. He works as an electrician for local government and has access to a day crèche. As Carol increases her managerial responsibilities at work, certain tensions are emerging at home, partly through differences in earning capability. There are limited career moves for Carol now as the managerial positions above her increase in status but decrease in number. She is hoping for a change in responsibilities which could offer increased challenge.

Diane is coming out

Diane is taking an open learning course with her local college in desk top publishing. She is preparing a business plan and doing market research to explore the possibilities of her idea further.

DISCUSSION POINTS

1. What are the similarities between marketing yourself on the jobmarket and the selling process in general?

2. How relevant is your working life to the rest of your life?

3. What are the salary structures for your trade or profession in relation to a man doing the same work?

10
Preparing for Success

DEFINING SUCCESS

Measuring success is a relative operation. Success means something different to each one of us. It could mean:

- public recognition

- a big car

- money to spare

- standing in the community

- our children doing well

- passing our driving test

- acceptance

- a big house

- having a book published

- money in the bank

- parental acknowledgement

- getting promotion.

What does it mean to you?

One of the problems with success is that we are rarely satisfied with it. When we have achieved what we thought we wanted, we move the goalposts a little and set ourselves another target to reach for. In some ways, this is a good thing because we constantly challenge and stretch ourselves. We fulfil our potential. However, more often than not, we feel a sense of dissatisfaction. We've got 'there', but somehow it's not enough, it isn't quite as we thought. This is because we mistake an external measurement of success for the real thing of inner acceptance and contentment.

One of the hidden agendas in the search for success is the need to be noticed, approved of and accepted by others (primarily parents or other important role models). Often we are driven to achieve by a need to possess. But of course, when we possess, there is the danger of losing what we believe we possess. So we become fearful and possessive. Then we are stuck – afraid to move on in case we lose 'it', afraid to step back to become nothing once more. We are stuck.

Success is a constantly moving state. We tend to measure it by external representation – a good job, a nice home, a better car, well behaved children. When these external states change, our sense of achievement changes. In reality, all of what happens 'out there' is subject to being influenced by several factors, only one of which is ourselves.

Success could be our ability to:

● survive

● laugh

● learn new skills

● care for ourselves

● gain something positive from every situation

● love one another

● feel and express emotions

● continuously change

● feel powerful

● experience life.

Success in work, other than mastering your job-specific skills, is your attitude, your developmental skills, your perseverance, your openness, your compassion, your co-operation and facilitation skills. In essence, your success is your femaleness.

This book has been written to open you up to yourself and your potential. What follows is a brief reminder of the main points you have been reading.

PLANNING YOUR CAREER

There are a number of important facets to planning your career which you need to be aware of.

New ways to work

Gone is the 9-5, five days a week, job for life. As we approach the end of the millennium, we are expanding into new ways of working including contract work, jobsharing, flexitime and an increase in self-employment. Flexibility is the key word to surviving in a multi-career workplace.

You can expect to have more than one job at a time. They may be similar or they may be totally different from one another.

Multiple careers

Approximately every five years you are likely to change career direction. This is a reflection of personal changes and economic trends.

Working trends

The trend is going more to outsourcing work. As the core of a company shrinks to just key management and developmental workers, there are likely to be changes in the way the product or service of a company is delivered. Companies will outsource contracts to self-employed personnel or will provide work to a temporary workforce when demand arises.

IDENTIFYING YOUR ROLE MODEL

We learn by example. We learn from our parents, our siblings, our friends. We learn from pop stars, footballers, politicians, from those who represent important posts within the community. We learn how to behave, think and feel by observing those around us.

We learn how to operate in business by watching those in authority or those who are seen to be doing well. Normally men, occasionally women. Well known role models may include Richard Branson, the Princess of Wales, Michael Heseltine, Anita Roddick, Charles Handy. They have their good and bad points. We emulate particular behaviours according to how we want to feel, the reaction we want from others and a need to be approved of and accepted.

Women's image of themselves
Women tend to think they should emulate male behaviour in business. Therein lies the danger of becoming the female man.

Maybe we need to rethink our image and beliefs about ourselves as women in general and then build onto this, new values about women at work. Each gender has its own unique qualities. Each gender has an image of itself, perpetrated by itself. Each gender has expectations of the other.

In reality, although each gender has its peculiarities, each person also has individuality regardless of gender. It is by resourcing this uniqueness in ourselves, by accepting the uniqueness of another (gender or person), that we can express potential.

Balancing male and female
It isn't a matter of copying the male behaviour to cover the female. Neither is it a matter of raising female behaviour to discard the male. Success is about honouring and balancing the two.

CHOOSING POWER

When you express yourself, you are expressing your power. Your thoughts, feelings and behaviour express the real you. As we grow wiser, we begin to understand the real us. Not the defensive, angry, fearful, puffed-up us. But the loving, active, nurturing, logical, intuitive and decisive us. The self that is a balance of male and female.

Seeking approval
When we are young, we seek approval from our parents. We want them to notice us because then we feel important and acknowledged. We want them to approve of us because this means they love us. When we feel loved, we are accepted and we belong. Some of our most primitive urges come from the need to be accepted and loved. These urges can stay with us most of our lives and can even force their way into our working lives. We can subtly transfer these needs and drives onto authority figures in

the workplace. Our boss becomes our parent. We can become the child again, feeling powerless and vulnerable while giving away our power to the authority figures.

Taking risks

A child is frightened to take a risk in case the parent disapproves of the action. In order to take a risk, we have to overcome the fear of rejection, of appearing stupid or feeling embarrassed. We need to take responsibility for our thoughts, feelings and behaviour by becoming our own parent. Part of us can feel fearful but the parental part of our nature can reassure and encourage. We can take a risk while feeling fearful.

We can be in a work situation and feel in control. We may not want positions of authority but we do have personal status regardless of our company position.

Self-esteem

As we take risks and realise that we can survive the mistakes, the embarrassment and the success, we become more confident. Success breeds success.

Empowerment

Power is looking at the mighty oak that stands tall, spreading its branches and shading with its leaves.

Empowerment is becoming the mighty oak, feeling the roots penetrating the earth, feeling the security, solidity and strength of the tree as it reaches upwards and outwards.

BEING SKILFUL

Most people tend to think of skills as something they get paid for. However, we are developing and using skills all of the time – in paid and unpaid work. Work around the home, favours done for family and friends, voluntary work in our spare time and hobbies are all skills-based.

Being able to transfer skills from one area of your life to another, from unpaid to paid or from paid to paid work, is a crucial component of staying in work.

Job-specific skills

The better equipped you are in job-specific skills which can be transferred from occupation to occupation, the more likely you are to stay in work. It is to your advantage to develop your skills continuously and learn new ones, either on the job or in your own time.

Interpersonal skills

Almost as important as job-specific skills are interpersonal skills. Being able to communicate effectively with work colleagues and with customers and clients is increasingly more important. Being seen as assertive and able to interact with confidence will improve your own self-esteem as well as your opportunities in the workplace.

Additional skills

Bolt-on skills such as flexibility, information gathering, diversification, selling and negotiating, working in teams, autonomy, thinking skills, learning and study skills are all relevant in the employment marketplace today.

TRAINING YOURSELF FOR THE JOB

If you are returning to the workplace or wanting to change direction, consider the following steps:

● research the potential growth areas in commerce and industry

● assess your job-specific skills

● assess your work motivations

● see where your interests and inclinations fit in with the growth areas

● research opportunities and salaries

● explore the training routes, taking into account costs, childcare and study-time.

BREAKING THROUGH

A good manager of others manages herself just one step better. If you have aspirations to management, you need to learn self-development. If you aspire to be in charge of staff, developmental projects or your own business, you need to understand the way you think, feel and behave.

Having the job-specific skills and knowledge is only half the story. The other half is developing your potential, using your interpersonal skills and channelling your power constructively.

DEALING WITH SEXUAL HARASSMENT AND PREJUDICE

You are a human being, who happens to be a woman, who is also a sexual person. You work with other human beings, who happen to be men, who are sexual people. You are all working for a company doing a job. No one is there to win a popularity contest, but to get on with doing a job for money. Hopefully you enjoy what you are doing and you get along with others and others get along with you. But it doesn't always come together like that.

You may find yourself in a situation where a man is sexually harassing you. Coping tactics might include:

- confronting the harasser

- getting support from other women

- getting support from your union

- getting support from your superior

- contacting the Equal Opportunities Commission.

Get support and confront the harasser

You may find male colleagues snipe and bitch at you. You may find women colleagues snipe and bitch at you. You may do the same yourself. You may find prejudice from men and women. Coping tactics might include:

- being assertive and standing up for yourself

- looking at your own prejudices

- ignoring the comments and getting on with the job

- getting support from your superior.

Maintain your self-respect and be proud of your skills and knowledge.

BALANCING YOURSELF

As women enter the workplace in increasing numbers, they are still partially bound in their more traditional roles. As the emergence and re-balancing continues, we need to make sure our mental, spiritual and physical well-being is cared for and nurtured.

Healing the damage of stress

Before we heal, we need to be aware what it is that we are healing. We need to know:

● physical stress symptoms

● psychological stress symptoms

● stress-prone beliefs

● work pressures.

While a certain amount of stress is beneficial and can provide the adrenaline to act, too much stress can cause fatigue, apathy and illness.

If we are to effectively balance our lives to our satisfaction and well-being, we need to have a toolbox of coping strategies at our disposal including:

● time management

● getting out of our head into our bodies using exercise

● daydreaming

● physical relations techniques

● time for leisure and hobbies

● deep breathing

● healthy eating

● doing nothing

● saying yes

- good nutrition

- seeing friends

- sleeping

- doing something purely for the pleasure of doing it

- being able to shout and cry

- saying no.

DELEGATING FOR SUCCESS

A successful working life is a balanced one. You can't do everything – sometimes you have to trust, let go and delegate to others. You need to use the skills you enjoy and do well and be in a position to develop new ones. There are jobs which you do, both paid and unpaid, which others can do better. Sometimes you will have to do them, but often you can give them to others.

**You do not need to prove yourself by doing everything.
You will still be needed if you let go and delegate.**

Writing this book has been an experience for me. As a woman in business, I felt I had a great deal of knowledge to contribute – but I also discovered I have a lot to learn.

My working history has been erratic and challenging. I originally thought I wanted to be a nurse, but I am still not entirely sure whether that was my desire or my mother's. I slipped into secretarial and administration work but couldn't stand working for anyone else. I temped for a while and the freedom and wide range of experience suited me. I married and went self-employed in my early 20s, but I was too immature, lacking in business skills and still very much tied to conditioning patterns to make a success. When I went self-employed the second time in my late 20s, I was much more aware of myself. I took my first professional qualification when I was 30. Now I am in my late 30s and I am beginning to get a sense for the first time of satisfaction in my working life.

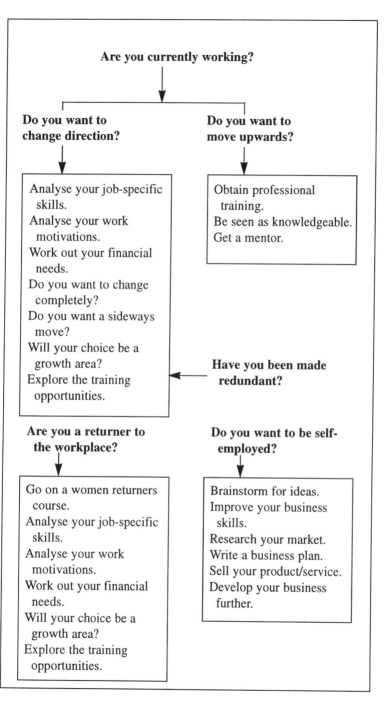

Fig. 20. Planning your career.

145

I have worked for and with women. Some have been vindictive behind my back, others have been openly encouraging, some have given me practical guidance and helped me move my career on. Most of my training courses in self-awareness have attracted women and I am grateful to those women for teaching me so much about my sex.

I have worked for and with men, negotiating and selling my training skills. I have negotiated the contents of this book with the male publisher. At present, I manage a training centre in career development. Most of the clients we train are men. I have run courses in a men's prison.

My experience has shown me that women tend to see each other as competitors but they do have sympathy for each other; women are anxious to learn but hold themselves back. When working with men, I have found them to be active and knowledgeable but hesitant to ask or take advice; men appear to be less sensitive to emotional content.

When a new piece of furniture is designed, it begins its creative journey in someone's mind. It is then given form on paper. It is sold to the decision-maker holding the purse strings, made into a prototype, then manufactured on a production line. Then it is made available for the public to purchase. We buy, place it in our home and get pleasure from it.

There is a process to all things. Whether it is a piece of furniture, a car, the birth of a child or the development of a business which creates employment – there are many stages involving different people. Each person contributes a uniqueness. Each facet of uniqueness creates the whole. Then we have success because we have worked together, bringing each part in. Men and women will work together because that is the way forward in business, commerce and industry – each part understanding and respecting the differences in the other.

Whatever you do in your working life, do it with a good heart. As much as possible, enjoy yourself. But as one man said to me 'above all, be yourself'. A woman in work. Good luck!

CASE STUDIES

Maria makes a decision

Maria wants to specialise in freelance video promotion in advertising. She expects to work erratic hours in a number of locations with people who are intense, argumentative and creative. If she is to survive, she understands that she is going to have to be assertive and quick. At this stage, success for Maria means work, money and moving into her own place.

Carol develops her skills

Carol is continuing to develop her management skills. During the time she has built up her work reputation, her private life has suffered, not necessarily as a direct result. Carol is learning how to reshape her emotional life and to draw her growing maturity into her work. She measures success by being true to herself. She is now considering retraining as a teacher in her late 30's.

Diane has designs for the future

Diane is setting up a desk top publishing and layout business from home, initially working for the printers she has just left. She will be working mainly for men on a freelance basis. She is beginning to measure success by her life experiences.

DISCUSSION POINTS

1. How do you measure success in your life?

2. Where would you like to be in five years from now with regard to work?

3. How has this book changed your perceptions of yourself as a working woman?

Glossary

Acupuncture. A form of natural medicine involving the meridian points in the body and the insertion of long, thin needles into them. The philosophy being that when discomfort occurs, there is an energy block along the lines and the needles are inserted to disperse the block.

Adult bursaries. Financial assistance available through your local careers office to assist with the cost of training.

Affirmations. A short, positive statement worded in the present tense which affirms (makes firm) the positive, Instead of 'I feel tense and worried' you could say 'I am alert and ready for anything.'

Anima. Jung evolved the theory that within every male is an energy force which represents the female side of his nature. The positive side of the anima keeps the man attuned to his inner values. A negative anima would show itself as irritability, depression, insecurity and uncertainty. Identifying completely with the anima may make a man effeminate or homosexual. The anima is responsible for man's image of women. A man will attract to him the outward personification of his anima.

Animus. The animus was also formulated by Jung and shows the male within woman. This image is responsible for woman's image of men. Over-identification with the animus may make a woman ruthless, domineering, cold and forceful. However, the animus can also build a bridge to creative activity. A woman will attract to her the outward personification of her animus.

Apathy. A state of boredom, of not wanting to be bothered.

Assignments. Vocational learning is partially based on assignments – projects which have a specified time for completion.

Autonomy. Freedom of action.

Bigot. Someone who is prejudiced.

Career Development Loans. An amount between £200 and £8,000 to pay for up to 80 per cent of course fees plus the full cost of books and materials. The course must be related to the work you want to do, it can be full or part-time and lasting no longer than two years.

Catalyst. A force for change.

Chiropractic. A natural health therapy for manipulating the back.

Coaching. Guiding someone through a set of instructions and experiences.

Collude. To knowingly or unknowingly work with someone to produce an outcome.

Competence. Knowledge or skill in a work-based activity.

Conditioning. The way in which we learn how to think, feel and behave from our parents and other important role models.

Corporate. Relating to the company – as in corporate image or philosophy.

Criteria. The set of demonstrated skills or knowledge required to fulfil an outcome.

Customer care. Looking after the customer or client, answering queries and dealing with problems.

Empower. To allow other people the right to self-expression. To encourage their emergence as an individual.

Emulate. To copy.

Ethos. A philosophy, belief system.

Externalise. To make known, to demonstrate through speech or behaviour, thoughts and feelings.

Facilitate. To guide other people to their own conclusions.

Gender reversal. Experiencing each other's roles in the workplace and at home.

Global marketing. The world is the marketplace.

Herbalism. A form of natural medicine whereby ailments are treated through tablets or liquid made from flowers, herbs, shrubs or trees.

Hierarchy. A tiered approach to who is in charge.

Holistic. The whole of a person – mind, body and spirit.

Homeopathy. A form of natural medicine whereby ailments are treated with natural resources.

Interaction. Separate parts or people, acting together.

Internalise. Holding thoughts and feelings inside of ourselves.

Internally validated. A certificate or diploma issued by a college or university but not relating to an outside awarding body.

Interpersonal skills. Communications skills.

Jobcentre. Government run centres situated in every major town offering jobs, careers guidance, training information and benefit advice.

Kudos. Glory, renown.

Lead body. The industry body which leads the way to setting up standards for training.

Mentor. An experienced and trusted adviser.

Millennium. A period of one thousand years.

Monotonic. A flat voice with no variance in pitch or tone.

Multi-skilling. Having experience in a number of different fields.

Non-verbal. Body language.

Osteopathy. A manipulative therapy of the bones.

Ownership. Taking responsibility for what we say, think, feel and do.

Portfolio person. Someone who has more than one career at a time.

Pro-active. Taking action instead of waiting until something happens to you.

Procrastinate. To defer action.

Psychometric testing. A series of mental tests designed to test aptitude and attitude for work.

Role model. Someone we can emulate.

Rote. Learning by repetition.

Self-development. Understanding the way we think, feel and behave.

Stereotype. The labels we give ourselves and each other.

Study skills. Reading, writing and learning skills relevant to education and training.

TEC. Training and Enterprise Councils offer training opportunities to businesses and individuals seeking to update their workplace skills.

Third age career. A new career, maybe self-employment or consultancy work that follows traditional retirement.

Vocational training. Training for work.

Workplace assessment. Assessment which occurs when we are in the workplace doing our job. Normally related to taking an NVQ.

Further Reading

BENEFITS

A Guide to Housing Benefit RR2. DSS.
A Guide to Income Support IB20. DSS.
Family Credit Claim Pack FC1. DSS.
One Parent Benefit CH11. DSS
Self Employed? FB30. DSS.
Unemployment Benefit NI12. DSS.
Voluntary and part-time Workers FB26. DSS.

CHILDCARE

Making Opportunities, Jane Hutt (NCVO Publications, 1992).

CAREER DEVELOPMENT

A Woman's Guide to Managing Men, Vicky Hibbert and Sue Baker (Bowerdean Publishing, 1995).
Build your own Rainbow, Barrie Hopson and Mike Scally (Mercury, 1991).
Careers and Occupational Information Centre (COIC), PO Box 348, Bristol BS99 7FE. Books and leaflets.
Changing Course, Maggie Smith (Mercury, 1989).
Changing your job after 35, Godfrey Golzen (Kogan Page, 1993).
Finding a Job with a Future, Laurel Alexander (How To Books, 1996).
Guidelines for the Redundant Manager, (British Institute of Management).
How to Return to Work, Ann Dobson (How To Books, 1995).
How to Start a New Career, Judith Johnstone (How To Books, 1994).
Job Ideas (COIC). PO Box 348, Bristol BS99 7FE.
Job Search Guide, CEPEC Ltd, Princes House, 36 Jermyn Street, London SW1Y 6DN. For executives and professionals.
Jobs for the Over 50s, Linda Greenbury (Piaktus 1994).
Just the Job, John Best (Nicholas Brealey, 1994).
Offbeat Careers, Vivien Donald (Kogan Page 1995).
She Who Dares Wins, Eileen Gillibrand and Jenny Mosley (Thorsons, 1995).
Test Your Own Aptitude, Jim Barrett and Geoff Williams (Kogan Page, 1990).

The Equality Myth, Kerry Chater and Roma Gaster (Allen & Unwin, 1995).
Women Mean Business, Caroline Bamford and Catherine McCarthy (BBC, 1991).
Working in –, (COIC), PO Box 348, Bristol BS99 7FE.

HEALTH

Instant Stress Cure, Lyn Marshall (Century Hutchinson, 1988).
Visualization for Change, Patrick Fanning (New Harbinger Publications, 1988).

FUNDING

Department for Education, Publications Centre, PO Box 2193, London E15 2EU. Tel: (0181) 533 2000. Information on grants.
MRC. Project grants, 20 Park Crescent, London W1N 4AL. Research and training opportunities and project grants.
Sponsorships 1995, COIC, Department CW, ISC05, The Paddock, Frizinghall, Bradford BD9 4HD.
Student Loan Company Ltd, 100 Bothwell Street, Glasgow G2 7GD. Tel: (0345) 300 900. Booklet on loans to students.
Tax Relief for Vocational Training, Personal Taxpayers Leaflet IR 119 (Inland Revenue).
The Grant Register (Macmillan Press).

HARASSMENT AND PREJUDICE

How to Know your Rights at Work, Robert Spicer (How To Books, 1991).
Making Advances, Liz Curtis (BBC, 1993).
Sexual Harassment in the Workplace: A guide for employers, ISCO 5, The Paddock, Frizinghall, Bradford BD9 4HD.

NEW WAYS OF WORKING

Changing Times (New Ways to Work, 1993).
Directory of Jobs & Careers Abroad, Alex Lipinski (Vacation Work).
Guide to Working Abroad, Godfrey Golzen (Daily Telegraph/Kogan Page, 1994).
Job Sharing: A Practical Guide, Pam Walton (Kogan Page, 1990).
National Council for One Parent Families, 255 Kentish Town Road, London NW5 2LX. Tel: (0171) 267 1361. A guide is available helping in various ways.

POSITIVE THINKING

Creative Visualisation, Shakti Gawain (Bantam, 1985).

Open University Validation Services. Tel: (0171) 278 4411.
Periodicals Training Council. Tel: (0171) 836 8798.
Photography and Photographic Processing Industry Training Organisation. Tel: (0121) 212 0299.
Pitman Examination Institute. Tel: (01483) 415311.
Publishing Qualifications Board. Tel: (0171) 278 4411.
Refrigeration Industry Board. Tel: (0181) 647 7033.
RSA Examinations Board. Tel: (01203) 468080.
Scottish Vocational Education Council. Tel: (0141) 248 7900.
Sea Fish Industry Authority. Tel: (01482) 27837.
Security Industry Training. Tel: (01905) 20004.
Telecommunications Vocational Standards Council. Tel: (01908) 265500.
Vocational Training Charitable Training. Tel: (01243) 842064.

TRAINING (FUNDING)

Career Development Loans, Freepost, PO Box 99, Sudbury, Suffolk CO10 6BR. Freephone (0800) 585505.
Department of Health, Student Grants Unit, Morcross, Blackpool FY5 3TA. Tel: (01253) 856123. Grants for occupational therapy, physiotherapy, radiography, dentistry.
Educational Grants Advisory Service, Family Welfare Association, 501–505 Kingsland Road, London E8.
Local Education Authorities (LEA), local *Yellow Pages*. Mandatory and discretionary grants.
Project 2000, local health authority. Bursaries for nursing.

TRAINING (INFORMATION)

ECCTIS 2000, Fulton House, Jessop Avenue, Cheltenham, Gloucester GL50 3SH. Tel: (01242) 518724. Computer databases found in colleges, careers offices, adult guidance services and libraries giving information on around 100,000 courses in the UK.
National Council for Vocational Qualifications, 22 Euston Road, London NW1 2BZ. Tel: (0171) 728 1893.
Training Access Points (TAPS), St Mary's House, c/o Moorfoot, Sheffield S1 4PQ.

TRAINING (OPEN LEARNING)

Educational Liaison Officer, Channel 4 Television, 60 Charlotte Street, London W1P 2AX. Learning from home via the TV.
Insight Information, BBC, Broadcasting House, London W1A 1AA. Learning from home via the TV.

National Extension College, 18 Brooklands Avenue, Cambridge CB2 2HN. Tel: (01223) 316644. Study skills, GCSEs, A levels, degrees, professional studies and languages.

The Open College, St Paul's, 781 Wilmslow Road, Didsbury, Manchester M20 8RW. Tel: (0161) 434 0007. Work-related courses including work skills, management and supervision, accountancy, health and care, technology and education and training.

Open College of the Arts, Houndhill, Worsbrough, Barnsley, South Yorkshire S70 6TU. Tel: (01891) 168902. Art and design, creative writing, drawing, garden design, music, painting, photography, sculpture and textiles.

The Open University, PO Box 71, Milton Keynes MK7 6AG.

Radio Publicity, BBC, Broadcasting House, London W1A 1AA. Tel: (0171) 580 4468. Learning from home via the radio.

WOMEN'S DEVELOPMENT

Business and Professional Women UK, 23 Ansdell Street, Kensington, London W8 5BN. Tel: (0171) 938 1729.

Women Returners' Network, Euston House, 81-103 Euston Street, London NW1 2ET. Tel: (0171) 388 3111.

WORKING PARENTS AND CARERS

Parents at Work, 77 Holloway Road, London N7 8JZ. Tel: (0171) 700 5771. National and local support, publications.

Black and Ethnic Minority Childcare Working Group, Wesley House, 4 Wild Court, London WC2B 5AU.

Carers National Association, 29 Chilworth Mews, London WC2 3R. Tel: (0171) 724 7700. Information and network.

National Association of Carers, 58 New Road, Chatham, Kent ME4 4QR.

National Childminding Association (Childminding – in business), 8 Masons Hill, Bromley, Kent BR2 9EY. Tel: (0181) 464 6164. Networking.

Kid's Club Network, 279-281 Whitechapel Road, London E1 1BY. Tel: (0171) 247 3009. Information and development on setting up after-school and holiday clubs.

Working Mothers' Association, 77 Holloway Road, London N7 8JZ. Tel: (0171) 700 5771.

Index